BRIGHT NOTES

ANNA KARENINA BY LEO TOLSTOY

Intelligent Education

Nashville, Tennessee

BRIGHT NOTES: Anna Karenina
www.BrightNotes.com

No part of this publication may be used or reproduced in any manner whatsoever without written permission, except in the case of brief quotations in critical articles and reviews. For permissions, contact Influence Publishers http://www.influencepublishers.com.

ISBN: 978-1-645423-06-5 (Paperback)
ISBN: 978-1-645423-07-2 (eBook)

Published in accordance with the U.S. Copyright Office Orphan Works and Mass Digitization report of the register of copyrights, June 2015.

Originally published by Monarch Press.
Herbert Reaske, 1965
2019 Edition published by Influence Publishers.

Interior design by Lapiz Digital Services. Cover Design by Thinkpen Designs.

Printed in the United States of America.

Library of Congress Cataloging-in-Publication Data forthcoming.
Names: Intelligent Education
Title: BRIGHT NOTES: Anna Karenina
Subject: STU004000 STUDY AIDS / Book Notes

CONTENTS

1)	Introduction to Leo Tolstoy	1
2)	Textual Analysis	
	Part One	14
	Part Two	28
	Part Three	44
	Part Four	53
	Part Five	60
	Part Six	70
	Part Seven	81
	Part Eight	89
3)	Character Analyses	93
4)	Critical Commentary	102
5)	Essay Questions and Answers	108
6)	Bibliography	115
7)	Annotated Bibliography	117

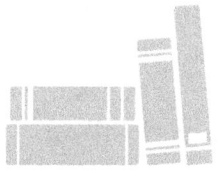

INTRODUCTION TO LEO TOLSTOY

THE LIFE AND CAREER OF LEO TOLSTOY

Count Leo Nikolayevich Tolstoy was born on August 28, 1828, on his father's estate of estate of Yasnaya Polyana, in the Province of Tula, Russia. The Tolstoys were a family of the old Russian nobility who served the Czars and ruled the Empire. He was a count who was raised in a large family in the best tradition of the nobility. He was orphaned by the time he was nine, and his education was taken over by an aunt. Tolstoy entered the University of Kazan in 1844, where he studied oriental languages and later law, but he left in 1847 without receiving a degree.

In his youth Tolstoy led the usual easy-going life of young men of his class - lighthearted and full of pleasure seeking. However, as his diary reveals, he was incapable of completely indulging himself in this kind of existence. He began at an early age to try to find a rational and moral justification of life - this quest remained the dominant force of his mind throughout his life and career.

In 1851, Tolstoy enlisted in the army as a volunteer and served until 1854, fighting guerrilla tribesmen in the Caucasus. Later, he served as an officer during the Crimean campaign, and was involved in the siege of Sevastopol. His Sevastopol Stories appeared while the siege was still on.

He began his literary career with stories of reminiscence: Childhood (1852), Boyhood (1854), and Youth (1856). These stories gained him his first fame and he was welcomed by the literary circles of Petersburg and Moscow. But Tolstoy was too much of an aristocrat to like these semi-Bohemian intelligentsia, whom he considered self-consciously plebian. In turn, they disliked his superior attitude. They could not appreciate the experimental value of his later works, so his association with the literary world was quite short-lived.

The years 1856–61 were divided between Petersburg, Moscow, Yasnaya, and foreign countries. His travels to Europe left him disgusted with the materialistic values of the bourgeois civilization. In 1859 he started a school for peasant children at Yasnaya and wrote a primer, graded reader, and arithmetic book, which had an enormous circulation. In 1860 he was profoundly affected by the death of his brother Nicholas (who appears as Nikolai in *Anna Karenina*). This was Tolstoy's first encounter with the inevitability of death.

In 1862, he married Sophie Andreyevna Behrs. Tolstoy married her when she was eighteen and he was thirty-four. He had known her as a child and at one point had been practically engaged to one of her sisters. She was the loveliest of the daughters of Dr. Behrs, a prominent and highly successful physician. Tolstoy had made a point of not marrying into his own social class, because he had lost respect for it after a dashing and dissolute youth as a wealthy Barine (baron). By the time of his marriage, Tolstoy was no longer living in the big mansion at Yasnaya Polyana, because a series of high escapades and various army posts had left him in debt. He had been forced to sell it for the value of the bricks and other building materials.

The "little" white house at Yasnaya Polyana where Tolstoy brought his wife the day after the wedding was soon too small for the growing family. (The Tolstoys had a total of thirteen children.) Tolstoy kept adding wings and extensions. Tolstoy had to send for an English governess eventually. This situation was difficult for the young mother, who did not know English. However, her fluency in other languages proved a boon. Yasnaya Polyana was a multilingual center. The senior Tolstoys, like many of the Russian nobility, spoke a great deal of French together, and they knew Russian and German as well. Besides the footmen, the coppersmith who made and repaired samovars, the cook and the cook's son, the stablemen, the grooms, the shepherds, the agents, and the laundress, there was the favorite Alexei, the writer's personal servant who had been with Tolstoy ever since he and his brother were orphaned.

In addition to the permanent residents, there was always a conglomeration of relatives on long visits. (We are reminded of Dolly's visits to Levin in *Anna Karenina*.) Visitors came frequently for special entertainments and amateur theatricals.

In the winter there were fancy dress balls which were less sophisticated than similar parties in St. Petersburg or Moscow. Regardless of the demands of his writing, there were periods when Tolstoy would sit down for three hours a day and play the piano. Other times he would steal time, and rescue the children from their studies to teach them to ride bareback. Summers, the family would take short trips on foot or in carts to bathing spots. At harvest time, Tolstoy would spend the whole day in the fields where he would take his place in the line of reapers.

The other nobles of the area criticized him strongly for this. In *Anna Karenina* there are several scenes where Levin (Tolstoy) participates in the work of the farm. There are also hunting scenes. Tolstoy could not forego a chance to go bird hunting when an old friend, brother, or guest came down for a shoot.

Amid the flurry of activity with the estate and his growing family, Tolstoy created two gigantic literary masterpieces. The peculiarities of his art are most spectacularly revealed in *War and Peace*, the creation of which took seven years (1862–8). It is a historical novel on a grandiose scale, unfolding the panorama of European events between 1805 and 1814, giving a detailed picture of Napoleon's campaign in Russia in 1812.

Anna Karenina, a novel of family life and contemporary manners, began in 1873. The first installments appeared in 1875, and the publication of the novel was completed in 1877. *Anna Karenina* leads up to the moral and religious crisis that was to revolutionize Tolstoy's entire life. Before he began to write it, he had already been thinking about new artistic methods - abandoning the psychological and analytical manner of superfluous detail and discovering a simpler narrative style that could be applied not only to the sophisticated and corrupt educated classes, but to the undeveloped mind of the people. Tolstoy's writings after 1880 are divided by a deep cleft from all his earlier work. By 1880 his so-called "conversion" was complete. He was no longer interested in producing literature, but in conveying a moral and religious message. He now preached a primitive Christianity purged of ritual, church organization, and priesthood. The important thing was that men should love one another. In *My Confession* (1879), he described his personal "transformation," a kind of mystic fervor combined with a glorifying of work. In *What Is to Be Done?* (1884), he attacked the evils of money and the life of the leisured and professional classes. In *What is Art?* (1897), he denounced art for art's sake, attacked many of the world's greatest writers, and insisted on religion and social purpose as the test of all art. He rejected his own greatest works. But he continued to write fiction, *The Kreutzer Sonata* (1889), a study of jealousy and a diatribe against sexual education of young men and women, and *Resurrection* (1899), a long novel which reflected his negative attitude toward society.

After his conversion, Tolstoy became increasingly identified with religious populism - union and communion with working people as the moral and religious solution to all problems. He became alienated from his wife and children, who considered him an eccentric mystic. He renounced his own class, turned vegetarian, reduced his material needs to a minimum, and even renounced his copyrights. This religious populism ran parallel to the revolutionary social populism of the radical intelligentsia in Russia, which led to the downfall of Czarism just seven years after his death. Tolstoy caught pneumonia and died at Ostapovo, an obscure railroad station, on November 20, 1910. He was buried at Yasnaya Polyana.

THE WRITING OF ANNA KARENINA

The novel was slow in its conception and even slower in being written. Tolstoy, not long after the publication of *War and Peace*, which put him in the limelight of world literature, had an idea to write a novel about a woman in high society who deceives her husband. But he soon discovered that being a well-known figure was time-consuming. His correspondence was great. He was still a wealthy count with an estate to manage. His old interest in education did not flag. Accordingly, it was three years later, in 1873, when he really started on *Anna Karenina*. Another three years passed, and in December, 1876, Tolstoy's wife wrote to her sister, "We are at last writing *Anna Karenina* as it should be written; that is without interruption. Full of energy, concentrated, Lyovochka (the endearing diminutive name for Leon, Leo, or Lev) adds a whole chapter each day while I recopy as fast as my fingers can write; at this present, while I am writing to you, the pages of my letter cover the pages of the chapter he wrote yesterday... ."

One must smile at her writing "without interruption." This amazing couple had thirteen children by 1888. Sophie, who copied *War and Peace* several times and went through all the drafts of *Anna Karenina*, once wrote that she was either pregnant or nursing the entire time. Sergei, Tolstoy's oldest son, has given us a clear picture of life at Yasnaya Polyana during the time when his father was writing *Anna Karenina*. His book, Tolstoy Remembered, was not translated into English and published (London) until 1961, more than fifty years after the great writer had died. Sergei's record of their life at this time is an expansive kaleidoscope of people, making one appreciate the skill with which Tolstoy wove so many of them into his writing, particularly in *Anna Karenina*.

The hint of bitterness that was to dominate much of Tolstoy's later writing is beginning to be evident in *Anna Karenina*. In the same sense there are indications of Tolstoy's religious "conversion," which possibly brought him more fame than *War and Peace* and *Anna Karenina*. The last chapters of *Anna Karenina*, we must remember, were written much later than the first. Tolstoy, who was famous for his many corrections and revisions, always regretted that he had started to put the opening books of *Anna Karenina* into print before the end was written. To be sure, he had outlined it in full detail nearly a year in advance of his agreement with the Russian Herald for serial rights.

Life had done much to change the author's viewpoint between February 1870, when he spoke of writing about "a woman who is married in high society, but who ruins herself," and January 1875, when the first installment appeared. For one thing, a close neighbor, Anna Pirogova, committed suicide by throwing herself under a train in June, 1872. In mid-May, 1873 he put aside the draft to take time to visit Samara (the second estate he owned) where the suffering of the Bashkirs as a result of drought aroused his sympathy; he raised nearly two million rubles and provided over 750,000 pounds of wheat for their relief.

In.that same year, in November, he lost the first of his infant children. (He was to lose two more in as many years after.) The death of the eighteen-month-old Peter had a very sobering effect on the course of his authorship. He wrote, "One may take consolation in the fact that if one had to choose one of us eight, this death is the easiest of all and for all to bear; but a heart, especially that of a mother, is a wonderful manifestation of the Divinity on earth, it does not reason, so my wife is much stricken."

His sorrow was converted into a drive to work. He worked with extreme intensity. When he went back to *Anna Karenina*, he little realized how much work there was ahead of him. As a result of his laborious productive effort, he slumped off as soon as the opening pages were in print. The reviewers were enthusiastic but he claimed he was disgusted and bored. Instead of a further work cure, he took the summer off and went to Samara where he not only bought horses, but, to the delight of the Bashkirs, organized horse races. Sometimes a thousand tribesmen watched a single race.

Back home in the fall, his wife became gravely ill, giving birth prematurely to a little girl who lived only long enough to be christened. The next month, the old aunt who had brought him up died. Her death had the effect of regarding Tolstoy's evolution towards faith. The old lady had gone to her death, fearing and fighting it. To the end she maintained a lack of humility and insubordination to the will of God. Undoubtedly this attitude of hers affected Tolstoy's account of Nikolai's death. In February 1876, after the beginning, but before the completion of *Anna Karenina*, Tolstoy wrote; "I do not believe in anything that religion teaches us to believe in; yet at the same time I not only hate and scorn unbelief, I cannot see any possibility of living without faith, much less dying without one. So I am gradually building up my beliefs but they are all, even if firm, still very indefinite, lacking in distinctness and the capacity for consolation."

A month before this, he had written to his brother: "Nothing is left in life but to die. I feel this constantly." This reminds us of the scene where Levin speaks of "hiding the rope."

Although *My Confession* was not published until 1879, it is unquestionable that Tolstoy was going through a religious evolution during the writing of *Anna Karenina*. Because Tolstoy asks, through the mouths of so many characters, the eternal questions of all ages, the popularity of *Anna Karenina* continues.

TOLSTOY THE EDUCATOR

In addition to his educational work with peasants mentioned earlier, Tolstoy also spent a great deal of time on his children's education. He read to them regularly. He taught them mathematics, for which he devised a new method of multiplying. This system is similar to the contemporary "new math," now popularly called the "base five" concept. Instruction in the languages became the mother's province. Later, a German tutor was hired for the boys. Even so, Tolstoy took a hand especially when they participated in local exams. At one time he learned Greek to help his oldest son but became so interested in the Greek way of life that he altered many of his own viewpoints. These alterations are reflected in *Anna Karenina*.

While working on *Anna Karenina*, Tolstoy went ahead with the educational book, *The Alphabet*.

He had tried setting up a school for the peasants at Yasnaya Polyana. He experimented with the Lancaster method. One winter his older children were entrusted with the education of the peasant children, who came to the house where they crowded the rooms and halls. Regardless of the shrieks and laughter the experiment was considered successful. In 1862, he published a pedagogical magazine, *Yasnaya Polyana*, in which he shocked his readers by contending that it was not intellectuals who should teach peasants, but vice versa.

TOLSTOY AND THE PEASANTS

From his childhood until his death, Tolstoy always saw agricultural work as man's means of providing all his needs. The **theme** of work is dominant in Tolstoy, particularly in *Anna Karenina*. Because of the influence of German medicine in Russia, Tolstoy took up the name Arbeitskur (Labor Cure). He felt that physical exercise insured a healthy body and a healthy mind. Tolstoy himself enjoyed good health. Even when he was "sick" after a long winter of indoor study, writing, and waiting on ailing children and a tire-out wife, he took a Kumiss cure by going down to Samara for a "rest" - "Rest" meant horseback riding, sleeping outdoors, examining property and digging for ancient ruins!

Tolstoy had, like most naturally healthy people, little patience with sickness. His own brother's sickness and death are mirrored in the harrowing account of Levin's brother, Nikolai. Tolstoy's evolution from a fear of death to an acceptance of death as a fact of life, even as an adventure not necessarily to be shunned, represents a major part of the fabric of *Anna Karenina*. Tolstoy always admired the peasant's simple confrontations with life and death.

At one time Tolstoy tried to free the serfs. As a young intellectual he had always believed that slavery was immoral, that the salvation of the Russian economy rested on an agriculture maintained by free labor, and that only through education could the serf learn responsibility. As the landowner, Tolstoy went to a great deal of trouble in his attempt to get the serfs to accept their freedom. He made various arrangements by which they could obtain land through token payments of a few rubles each year over an extended period. The peasants, however, were suspicious and refused. They loved him as a man, but not as a member of his class. **Irony** lies in the fact that, intellectually, Tolstoy was an anarchist. Believing in the complete absence of government, he contended that government by its very nature engendered corruption. An official could not avoid dishonesty. Late in life Tolstoy gave away all his property.

TOLSTOY AS INNOVATOR

Tolstoy's enthusiasm for life is infectious. All the characters and their activities in *Anna Karenina* are interesting. The author's genius makes not only the extraordinary but the commonplace meaningful. The most complicated personality, even Anna herself, gains clarity when placed alongside a peasant who chews a wisp of hay at the roadside. Tolstoy was forever curious about the whole person, and the whole person was more than a list of personality traits an author might jot down. The heart often transcends reason. That mankind is weak, as well as strong, is a primary fact of life Tolstoy never forgot. His characters are revealed by two distinct methods.

In the first instance, his masses of characters are revealed in their relationships with each other. We see them at large dinner parties, at the opera in between the acts, at the races, in railroad stations, in military barracks. Their outward movements and their public and social faces tell tales about their inner souls. Opposed to this restless, yet formalized, motion picture of life, Tolstoy sets the still slide of a single individual. Here he is an innovator, along with other nineteenth century figures such as Balzac and Dostoevsky. For an author to climb inside his characters and do their soul searching was new to the novel. In a sense Tolstoy has his characters think out loud for the reader's benefit. Tolstoy was criticized for this. It was said that his people are too introspective. Their inner disputations disturb the flow of action in the story too frequently. These halts are indeed noticeable, in particular with the autobiographical character of Levin. On the other hand, the personality of Anna grows with her struggles and the personality of Count Vronsky, her lover, shrinks for the lack of them.

SUMMING UP

War and Peace, which was Tolstoy's gigantic novel that preceded *Anna Karenina*, established his reputation. It is usually accorded the distinction of being the best of Tolstoy. There are many who dispute this, preferring *Anna Karenina*. Some reasons are obvious. In the first place *Anna Karenina* is free of the long military passages in *War and Peace* that seem dull to many readers. In the second place it is contended that *War and Peace* holds itself in first place because it was first in time.

Immediately after *Anna Karenina*, Tolstoy experienced his so-called religious "conversion." The novels that followed this change revealed Tolstoy primarily as a humanist, philosopher and commentator on the contemporary scene, rather than as an artist. Because there was a hint of this "conversion" toward the end of *Anna Karenina*, there is an easy tendency to link it with the later books. On the other hand it should be remembered that the strength of *War and Peace*, which rests on the author's magnificent panorama of the Russian nobility and the people who lived on the fringes of such society, is redoubled in *Anna Karenina*. The marriages and the family life of the three women give the later novel a unity and artistic structure lacking in the first book. In addition, the fact that one of the marriages is a representation of the author's own lends support to its **realism** and enhances its interest.

It is to be remembered that Tolstoy wrote for his own class, aristocrats who read Dickens and Jane Austen, Flaubert and Gautier, Schiller and Goethe in the original languages. It is ironic that he did not write for the common man who is now his strongest admirer-so much so that new translations are continuously appearing in most languages. The books that have been written about Tolstoy fill many shelves on university libraries. So many books certainly represent a divergence of opinion. Fortunately for the book lover and poet, these tomes are more concerned with Tolstoy as a prophet, than as an artist. It must be admitted that as a prophet he is to be commended for his prediction of the Russian revolution. As a religious figure, he is also admired by many or his sense of pan-religionism, the Buddhistic views of Christianity which seem to be relevant to today's ecumenical perspectives.

A NOTE ON RUSSIAN NAMES

The title *Anna Karenina* sometimes becomes *Anna Karenin*. Anna's husband is Karenin. In Russian a is usually the feminine ending, but Karenin has become Karenina in translation. Accordingly, we have Mrs. or Madame Karenina. More usually she is called, Russian style, Anna Arkadyevna. This patronymic stems from her father's name, Arkady; thus she is Anna, daughter of Arkady. In the same sense, Anna's brother, Prince Oblonsky is called Stepan Arkadyevich. Fortunately the family nicknamed him Stiva. It is also comforting to the English reader that Oblonsky's wife, the Princess Darya Alexandrovna Shcherbatsky is called Dolly. The masculine suffixes ovich, ievich (or ich and ych) are similar to the English prefixes Mac or O'. Feminine endings include ovna, ievna, and ishna.

In this novel there are many, many characters with difficult names. However, they are so clearly drawn, and they appear in the story so frequently that one has little trouble keeping them straight. Even at the opening the new names do not flood the pages, but are introduced in orderly sequence. By the end of part one, roughly page 125, each is an old friend, or enemy.

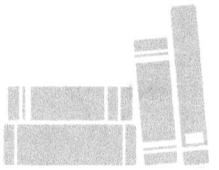

ANNA KARENINA

TEXTUAL ANALYSIS

PART ONE

CHAPTERS 1 THROUGH 6

The opening sentence, "All happy families are alike but an unhappy family is unhappy after its own fashion," sets the tone for the unhappy situation in which Prince Oblonsky finds himself when his wife learns of his affair with their children's French governess. It is a miserable situation, even vulgar, but the Prince says to himself, "What a governess!"

Oblonsky wakes up in his study where he has spent the night on a leather sofa. After recalling a delightful dream which took place in a German city in America, where he had sat down to a glass banquet table on which the shapely glass decanters had been women, he realizes suddenly why he has not been sleeping in his wife's bedroom. He is angry with himself, not so much for having fallen out of love with his wife, but for having been caught. He is a robust young man of thirty-four. His wife is about the same age, but she has had seven children and buried two. She has become faded and plain. He had thought that she had guessed his unfaithfulness before. Then, why this sudden outburst? For three days she has remained in her rooms. The children have been wandering about the house. The cook has left. The coachman has given notice. Everybody knows there is trouble in the house.

Oblonsky jumps up, strides over to the window, expands his chest and rings the bell vigorously. Matvey comes in bringing Oblonsky's clothes and a telegram. He is followed by the barber. After the Prince is shaved, dressed, and sprinkled with eau de cologne, he is less depressed. The telegram does not bother him. It is from his sister Anna. She is coming for a visit. He will tell Dolly (his wife) to get a room ready. Dolly! He will have to see her, talk to her, persuade her not to move out. Breakfast first.

Breakfast is pleasant and so is the liberal newspaper that goes with it. Oblonsky takes it, not because he prefers liberalism to conservatism but because liberalism better suits his way of life. Most of his circle is liberal. Liberalism is fashionable and Oblonsky chooses his opinions as he does a new hat or coat. Besides, in the section on political events he knows everyone who is mentioned - he reads that Count (in Russian imperial society counts ranked higher than princes) So-and-So has gone abroad, that there is no need for grey hair, that a light carriage is for sale. He is interrupted by two of his children who are playing coaches in the hall. They are screaming at each other in English. Tanyakin is his oldest daughter and favorite. He gives her a couple of bonbons.

"How is mamma?" he asks her.

Mamma? She is up," replies the girl who knows full well why she was asked the question.

Matvey announces that his carriage is ready, but Oblonsky realizes that he must talk to his wife. "I shall have to sooner or later."

When he enters her bedroom, Dolly is standing before an open chest of drawers. Articles are strewn all over; she is packing. She is sorting the children's clothes to take to her mother's where she knows the children will be worse off. One of them is sick, from sour broth. Impossible. She knows she won't be able to leave, but she must punish Stiva!

"Go away, go away, go away," she cries. When Stiva sees his wife's worn face and hears the notes of her despair, his eyes begin to moisten. He feels so sorry for her, but he fails to understand how his pity exasperates her. She gets more excited the more he begs her forgiveness. Finally, she goes out banging the door behind her.

Matvey asks if Oblonsky will be home for dinner. "It depends," responds the Prince, leaving.

Thanks to his natural ability at school, Oblonsky had learned easily. He was friendly. He was born into the circle of people who were in power or coming into it. Half Moscow and St. Petersburg are his relatives or relatives of his friends. Despite his youth and his dissipation, he has a distinguished post as head of one of Moscow's court houses. He has the job through Alexei Alexandrovich Karenin, Anna's husband, who is in the ministry. One looked after one's own and Oblonsky could perform his functions no worse than others.

Stiva has good qualities also. In his court job his indulgence with people is an asset. Perhaps he is mindful of his own shortcomings. His tendency to treat all men alike, regardless of status, is so genuine that it wins him respect. Lastly he is not emotionally involved in his work. His detachment prevents mistakes; he never makes them.

After a morning during which he sat in a session continuously until the two o'clock adjournment, Oblonsky is relaxing with his colleagues when he remembers that he had seen a man being ejected earlier from the courtroom. He summons the doorkeeper who soon sends in his old boyhood friend, Levin. He quickly surveys Levin's new suit which had obviously been tailored by a Frenchman. This new attention to attire, untypical of Levin, brings a smile to Oblonsky's face. Ah yes! Levin is in love with Kitty, Dolly's sister.

"I must have a talk with you," Levin says with agitation. He is all dressed up, in from the country where he does something or other Oblonsky never can understand. Levin's clothes do not conceal his lack of ease. His hurry is irritating; Levin is aware of the irritation and is angry with himself for causing it. He glances at the elegant hands of one of Oblonsky's colleagues-long, white fingers extended from large, glittering cuff links. Levin despises his friend's town life and official duties. How futile!

During the introductions that follow, Oblonsky is able to laugh with confident good humor while Levin, feeling more and more unsure of himself, frowns and shakes hands coldly. He recovers enough composture to ask after the Shcherbatskys. He does not mention Kitty. Oblonsky remembers his problem with Dolly. A secretary comes in with a sheaf of papers and a question. Oblonsky handles him with intelligence and efficiency.

After the secretary's withdrawal, Levin is more relaxed. Oblonsky says that his wife is not well, but if Levin wants to see the rest of the family, they will be at the Zoological Gardens at four. Kitty skates there. Oblonsky suggests that Levin should go and he will meet him there later for dinner.

CHAPTERS 7 THROUGH 12

On his arrival in Moscow that morning, Levin had gone directly to see his older half-brother, Koznyshev. Kosnyshev was with a professor of philosophy. Levin sat down to wait for the professor to go, but became interested in the discussion. Levin had read the articles on natural science to which they were referring, but had never connected biology with questions concerning the meaning of life and death. Listening, he noticed that the two men seemed to link the scientific to the spiritual, but every time he thought they were getting to the heart of the matter they retreated with subtle reservations, quotations and allusions. Soon he was impatient for the professor to go.

Levin wanted to tell his brother that he had come to Moscow to ask his advice about Kitty. When the professor had gone, Levin suspected a slight condescension on his brother's part, especially with reference to Levin's interest in farming. Koznyshev was not really interested in the estate they had inherited from their mother. It had never been divided and Levin managed it for both of them. Koznyshev asked about Levin's Zemstvo, because he had a keen interest in these local district councils of self-government, which were still new in the land. He attached great importance to them. But Levin had to admit that he had resigned-what took place at the meetings had often been ridiculous. Even though he had at first put his heart into the Zemstvo, he felt that the experiment was doomed to failure.

Koznyshev changed the subject to their other brother, who had turned up like a bad penny. Nikolai Levin had squandered almost all his fortune and had associated with horrible people. Koznyshev had paid off a large I O U for him; Nikolai had replied in a note, "I humbly beg you to leave me alone. That is the only favor I ask of my amiable brothers."

However, Levin could not forget Nikolai because he was sick. That part of him which was so excited at the prospect of seeing Kitty made him want to forget Nikolai, but his conscience bothered him. Koznyshev had no such sympathies; he was only afraid that Nikolai might stir up trouble between him and Levin. It was in such a mood of conflict that Levin had sought out Oblonsky to find Kitty.

At four o'clock Levin steps out of the sleigh that has brought him to the Zoological Gardens. Levin tries to keep calm, but when he sees Kitty on the steps at the far end of the skating rink, joy and terror seize him. She is chatting with an older woman when her cousin, Nikolai Slcherbatsky, spots him. Levin thinks the sun is approaching when Kitty skates toward him. She is unsteady on her skates. She seems more beautiful than ever when she asks Levin when he returned to Moscow and how long he is to stay. When he answers that the length of his visit depends on her, her growing reserve frightens him. He hires some skates and is in heaven as they skate along together. She says she would learn quickly if she were more on his arm. This remark gives him confidence and he again says something that seems to worry her. They meet her mother, the Princess Shcherbatsky, who is polite but Levin thinks her demeanor is chilly. She reminds Levin that he is welcome to attend one of her regular weekly parties that evening.

The Princess Kitty was eighteen years old when Levin fell in love with her. He had stayed close at hand for weeks in constant attendance, but then had fled before declaring his love. He was too shy to tell her that, at thirty-four, he had a past that might shock her. His feeling of unworthiness created his hesitation. He returned to his country estate and came back only when he was convinced that he could not face life without her.

When Kitty and her mother left the skating rink, the Princess Shcherbatsky was disturbed by the sudden reappearance of Levin. She did not approve of Levin's strange modern opinions, his awkwardness in society, and "his wild sort of life in the country, busy with cattle and peasants." On the other hand, Count Vronsky was charming, well born, very rich and intelligent - a dashing officer with a brilliant military career ahead of him. He was all the mother could desire for her youngest daughter; nevertheless, she was a little anxious. Was Vronsky merely paying court to Kitty, who she could see was already infatuated?

Oblonsky meets Levin at the park and, as agreed, takes him to dinner at the most fashionable restaurant of men-about-town. The bronze chandeliers, the mirrors, the gas-light, the painted hat check girl and the Tartar waiters bowing to Oblonsky are distasteful to Levin. He tells Stiva that three dozen oysters, clear soup Printaniere and turbot for two are no substitute for his preference for white bread and cheese. Oblonsky responds almost bluntly, "There is one thing I ought to tell you. Do you know Vronsky?"

CHAPTERS 13 THROUGH 22

Later that evening Levin arrives at the Shcherbatsky home ahead of the other guests. He sees Kitty alone and proposes- very shyly. Kitty, knowing what he is going to say long before he says it, breathes heavily and is enraptured. Then she remembers Vronsky. "No that cannot be…. forgive me," is her answer to Levin.

Disconsolate, Levin turns to go, but is trapped by the arrival of other guests. One of Kitty's friends, the Countess Nordson, with all the enthusiasm of a newlywed, wants the single girl to marry the fascinating Vronsky. She has known Levin for some time, and has found him an easy mark for fun in society. She is banteringly hostile to Levin when Vronsky is announced. Wearing a brand new uniform that is both simple and elegant, Vronsky goes up to the princess and then to Kitty. He is "a dark squarely-built man of medium height with an exceptionally tranquil and firm expression on his good-natured, handsome face."

After a few social banalities, the conversation turns to spiritualism and table turning. Taking the discussion seriously, Levin is obviously disgusted and watches for his chance to leave.

As he does so, he runs into Kitty's father who, he is delighted to discover, is just as cordial to him as ever. His last glimpse of the party is sorrowful because he catches a glimpse of Kitty, smiling and chatting amicably with Vronsky.

After the guests have gone, the old prince Shcherbatsky is talking to his wife. "What have you done? Why this: first of all, you are doing your best to hook an eligible young man, which will be the talk of Moscow, and with reason. If you give a party, then you ought to invite everyone, and not pick out possible suitors. Invite all the young bucks ... get a pianist and let them dance. But don't have the sort of thing we had tonight - don't hunt up suitors. It nauseates me, absolutely nauseates me; and you've gone on until you've turned the girl's head. Levin is a thousand times the better man. As for that Petersburg dandy - they turn them out by the dozen, all alike and all trash... . I see one man who has serious intentions - that is Levin; and I see a conceited popinjay who is only amusing himself."

Meanwhile, Vronsky's first concern after leaving the party was to settle the question of where to go to finish the evening. He was sick of the night spots, so he surprised himself by returning to his hotel where he ordered supper, enjoyed it, and went straight to bed and to sleep.

The next morning Vronsky is at the station to meet his mother. There he meets Oblonsky who has come to greet Anna. Both men are in a lighthearted mood and discuss taking up a subscription for a party for a favorite actress. Oblonsky abruptly changes the subject to Levin. Vronsky, who had not been impressed with Levin the night before, is somewhat disinterested; but when Oblonsky begins to praise him, telling Vronsky that Levin is in love with Kitty, the Count is very attentive. They discuss Levin's moodiness, neither man mentioning what occurs to both - that Levin was turned down by Kitty. This realization delights Vronsky, who feels like a conqueror.

At the train Vronsky sees a lady stepping out. His experience as a man of the world tells him at a glance that she is a member of the best society. He must have another look at her - "not because of her beauty, not on account of the elegance and unassuming grace of her whole figure, but because of something tender and caressing in her lovely face as she passed. As he looked around, she too turned her head... .In that brief glance Vronsky had time to notice the suppressed animation which played over her face... . It was as though her nature was so brimming over with something that, against her will, expressed itself now in a radiant look, now in a smile. She deliberately shrouded the light in her eyes but in spite of herself it gleamed... ."

Inside the compartment the Countess Vronsky greets her son, as Anna, having failed to find her brother, steps back in. Vronsky is pleased that the two women shared the compartment; they had entertained each other the entire trip. The Countess talked about her son and Madame Karenina about hers, an eight-year-old from whom she is parted for the first time. The old lady, a woman of the world who had had several love affairs since the death of her husband, lost her heart to Anna and was hoping Anna would see her in Moscow. Just as they were getting out, passengers who had gone onto the platform were running back into their compartments. There was a commotion because there had been an accident. Oblonsky saw it happen. A guard, either drunk or too muffled up against the frost, had not heard the train shunting back and had been crushed. Oblonsky is horror-stricken and moved particularly because the guard's wife had seen the mishap.

Later as she is leaving the station, Anna is both pleased and puzzled when she learns by chance from the stationmaster that Vronsky made a generous donation of two hundred rubles to the dead man's family.

Arriving at her brother's home, Anna is welcomed by the deluded Dolly. Dolly cannot forget that her sister-in-law is the wife of one of the most important officials in St. Petersburg and a grande dame in society. Anna tries to console Dolly by listening to her indictment of Stiva, whom she says she can never forgive. Anna explains that men are unfaithful, but their wives are sacred to them. Because she, as a sister, knows Stiva's capacity for letting himself be completely carried away by his feelings and for repenting as quickly, she advises Dolly to forgive him, "utterly as if it had never happened, had never happened at all."

Surprisingly, Stiva is home for dinner. Kitty is there too. Kitty is captivated by Anna's charm: Oblonsky tells Kitty that he saw Vronsky at the railway station. Anna, noticing Kitty's interest, tells her about her trip with Vronsky's mother, who had told her many fine things of Vronsky as a boy. But for some reason she fails to mention Vronsky's gift of two hundred rubles.

After a late dinner, Vronsky pays a call and stops in the lower hall to talk to Oblonsky about some dinner party arrangements. Anna catches a glimpse of him and she knew he saw her. In the drawing room Kitty explains the lateness of the call to herself by musing on the possibility that Vronsky has been to her home, and finding her out, has come on the chance that he might see her.

Within a few days there is a brilliant ball. Kitty stops on the flower-decked staircase flanked by powdered footmen in red livery. She is aware that she is looking her best in an elaborate gown of tulle. She looks for Vronsky to whom she has promised the first quadrille. When he comes to claim her, Anna has joined her. Anna is not in lilac, the color Kitty was sure she should have worn, but in a low-necked black velvet gown "which displayed her full shoulders and bosom that seemed carved out of old ivory." Anna, seeing Vronsky, immediately chooses a partner, ignoring Vronsky's bow completely.

"Why is she displeased with him?" wonders Kitty.

CHAPTER 23 THROUGH 33

Meanwhile Levin keeps trying to convince himself that it was inevitable that Kitty should choose Vronsky, who is so much more sophisticated. He decides to visit his brother Nikolai, who he feels is in reality no worse than the people who despise him. It is not his fault that he was born with a tempestuous nature and a kink in his soul. Determined to tell Nikolai what is on his mind, Levin goes to the cheap boarding house where Nikolai lives. He is not alone. Masha, the young woman he took from a brothel who now lives with him as his wife, is sitting on the couch. There is also a young man with a huge mop of hair who is some sort of agitator for a locksmiths' labor union. At first Nikolai is rude to Levin, but in an attempt to be gay he orders some supper and vodka. While waiting for the liquor, Nikolai is again irritable and deprecating about their half-brother's book. Levin, paying but partial attention, is perceptive enough to notice that the woman is devoted to the sick man whose rasping cough is heartrending.

"You are both in the wrong," says Levin getting back into the conversation. "You are more to blame according to the letter, and he (Koznyshev) according to the spirit."

When the food arrives, Nikolai drinks vodka from a tumbler. His remarks jump from one subject to another. His speech grows incoherent. After drinking still more vodka, he wants to go out somewhere. With difficulty, they finally put him, hopelessly drunk, to bed. Before Levin leaves, Masha promises to keep in touch with him and to get Nikolai to visit him in the country.

The next evening, when Levin arrives at his village's small station, sees his one-eyed coachman, recognizes his own upholstered sledge and his own horses, his self-dissatisfaction and his vague sense of guilt almost immediately melt away. He sees what had befallen him in Moscow in a different light. As he is being driven along, he resolves to give up any hope of happiness - such as marriage - to forego any low passions, to work harder than ever, and to allow himself even less luxury. By the time his old nurse, Agatha Mihalovna, has welcomed him back home and seen to all his comforts, Levin is already calling for a lantern so that he can inspect a newly-born calf. He is soon caught up again in the details of the work on his estate.

Later he tries to read a book in the study of the large old-fashioned house. It is comfortable and warm. His mother and father had long since died, but he is sentimental enough to continue to heat the entire house. He pauses to listen to the endless chatter of the old nurse. Before long his imagination peoples the rooms with a new family. His dreams about marriage differ from most of his class. To them marriage is but one of the numerous facts of social life. For Levin marriage is the principal thing in life. Renounce the idea?

The morning after the ball, Anna too was leaving Moscow. She was having an argument with herself. She was ashamed to tell Dolly why she was departing ahead of time, but she wanted Dolly to tell her sister Kitty to ignore Vronsky's evident infatuation with Anna. Even though she was happy that she was still able to fascinate a young man like Vronsky, Anna did not want to hurt Kitty.

Seated in the dimly lit sleeping car with her maid Annushka beside her, she wraps a rug around her knees and opens a book. After the train starts, there are all kinds of different noises. Outside a terrible blizzard rages. The compartment is stuffy. She stares at the book as though the pages were blank. She recalls the ball and the slavish look in Vronsky's eyes. During the mazurka, in spite of herself, she had shown him how happy he was making her. Does he feel ashamed too? What is there for her to be ashamed of? Nothing has happened. "What more can there be between me and that officer lad than there is between me and the rest of my acquaintances?"

She is glad when the train stops at an intermediate station. Annushka wakes up and is surprised that her mistress is going to leave the train to go out into the wind and snow. With delight Anna fills her lungs with the fresh frosty air, listens to the creaking boards of the platform, watches the figures of the passengers and railway attendants getting more and more covered with snow. As she is about to get back in the train, a man wearing a military overcoat steps close beside her. She instantly recognizes Vronsky. His remarks are polite, but Anna offers no replies. In his eyes is the same reverent ecstasy which she had seen the night before. She begs him to forget the mazurka. He explains that not a word, not a gesture, in fact nothing about her could he ever forget. She flees into the compartment. During the remainder of the night journey, the tensions that had tormented her before steadily increase.

The next morning Karenin is at the station to meet his wife. As he approaches, Anna notices things about him that had never bothered her before-his ears, his flat feet, the way he swings his hips. He is happy that he could take a half-hour from his duties to meet her. In reply to her questions about their son, Seriozha, he says the boy is fine, and then goes on rapidly to tell her that there are certain social calls she should make. Meantime Vronsky suddenly becomes aware of Karenin. "Ah yes! The husband." He realizes that he had only half believed in the man's existence. Nevertheless, while his German valet is taking care of his luggage, Vronsky makes a point of greeting Anna and her husband. Karenin is coldly formal. In spite of this, Vronsky appeals to Anna, "I hope I may have the honor of calling on you?"

"Delighted," Karenin replies in a matter-of-fact tone. "We are at home on Mondays."

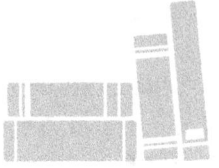

ANNA KARENINA

TEXTUAL ANALYSIS

PART TWO

CHAPTERS 1 THROUGH 9

Two months later Kitty's health becomes a family problem. After the family doctor had tried the usual remedies of cod liver oil and iron, a specialist, who was celebrated among the princess' set, is called in. Since he is still a young man, Kitty finds his examinations distasteful. Her father, who had little faith in doctors, listens to the medical discussions with contempt; the doctor has difficulty coming down to the level of the intelligence of this "old fool of a nobleman." The specialist, on a tip from the family doctor who knew that the princess wanted a trip abroad, finally recommends such a trip. However, he warns the princess not to trust to quacks; she should always refer any need to him.

Dolly, who had recently recovered after a confinement, calls to hear Kitty's fate after the consultation. She is unhappy, because Anna's suggestions about reconciliation with Stiva have not worked. He is little at home and money is scarce.

Dolly, despising her husband, despises herself more for being weak enough to allow herself to be deceived. She justifies her tolerance of his behavior by telling herself that she is holding the family together.

By the time Dolly arrives, the doctors have departed. The Prince and the Princess are at loggerheads. When the Princess begins to cry, the Prince regrets his outburst against the doctors and gives his wife a kiss. Kitty realizes that her father knows that her only troubles are those resulting from her disappointment over Vronsky. She is suddenly ashamed, chokes up in tears, and dashes from the room. Dolly soon follows her. She knows from Stiva that Levin had intended to propose to Kitty-she guesses that he actually did and that Kitty refused him. When she first tries to console Kitty, Kitty is disagreeable and says things she does not mean. In her anger she even hints at Stiva's unfaithfulness. This grieves Dolly. Before long both sisters have their faces buried in handkerchiefs. In a spirit of love and remorse, Kitty insists on helping her sister. One way is to help take care of one of Dolly's children who is suspected of having scarlet fever. All six children become ill, so it is Lent before the Shcherbatskys finally go abroad.

Meanwhile the exalted circle of St. Petersburg society notes a change in Anna Arkadyevna Karenina. This circle may be divided into three groups and Anna moves in them all. The first is her husband's official set. At the beginning of her marriage she had had almost a religious awe of these people, but later she learned who sided with whom and she lost interest. Another segment is dominated by the Countess Lydia Ivanovna. It consists of elderly, benevolent, pious women, and clever, learned and ambitious men. Karenin has the highest esteem for this group. Anna, before her trip to Moscow, had made friends here, but on her return finds its members insincere and generally unbearable. The third segment with which Anna has ties is society proper, "the world of balls, dinner parties, brilliant toilettes, which hung on to the court with one hand, lest it sink to the level of the demi-monde which the members of that fashionable world affected to despise, though their tastes were not similar but identical." Anna's link to this group was the Princess Betsy Tverskoy, her cousin's wife, who had an enormous income of 120,000 rubles and who had taken a great fancy to Anna. At first Anna had avoided the Princess Betsy and her coterie. On her return to St. Petersburg the situation changes. Disdaining her serious-minded friends, she cultivates high society. She sees Vronsky there, and experiences a tremendous excitement each time she meets him.

One evening before giving a party, the Princess Betsy is occupying her box at the opera. During the first intermission Vronsky calls on her. The two friends have a gay time; Vronsky describes a new role he has to play as mediator in a dispute between a minor official and an officer friend. His friend has been forward with the official's wife. Since there is no question of a duel, Vronsky can enjoy being slightly ribald in his account of the affair, especially when he perceives the Princess' pleasure. She urges Vronsky to stay for the opera, but he explains he is about to be off to some lighter music hall entertainment.

The Princess herself does not remain to the end of the performance. Even so, she is not home long before her guests arrive. In the drawing room of her huge house in Bolshaya Morskaya Street, the thick carpets, the white tablecloth, the silver samovar and the transparent china are gleaming in the candlelight. As hostess, she sits down by the samovar and takes off her gloves, while unobtrusive footmen arrange chairs for the guests. Various clusters of diplomats and titled people are formed, but the small talk has little variation. "Only what is spiteful is amusing." "We have got so tired of what is clever." Scandal seems to be the one ingredient that keeps conversation going.

"Anna is quite changed since her trip to Moscow."

"The great change is that she has brought back with her the shadow of Alexei Vronsky."

Shortly after these remarks, Karenin makes his appearance at the party. Since he knows everyone present, his entrance is disturbed with recollections of the attentiveness with which Anna and Vronsky talked together. He convinces himself that it would be insulting to Anna to appear as a jealous husband but he feels that he must talk to her since others may begin to make suggestive remarks. While waiting for her return, he prepares several little speeches to say to her. On her arrival, however, she upsets his preparations by pretending not to know what he is talking about. She is amazed at the ease with which she is willing to lie and deceive. This shocks her, but at the same time she is pleased with her private recollections of Vronsky.

CHAPTERS 10 THROUGH 19

What had been the one absorbing desire of Vronsky's life for nearly a year comes to pass. For him, this is the realization of total happiness. For Anna, unfaithfulness brings a sense of shame, rapture, and even horror. The complexity of her feelings is inexpressible. She keeps postponing the time when she will have to think things through. "By and by," she would say, "when I'm calmer."

Vronsky effortlessly he joins a group and immediately tells an ambassador's wife that he has been to the opera bouffe. He is about to make a comment on a certain French actress when he is interrupted by the Princess Myagky, who has learned that being outspoken is usually considered witty. The Princess remarks that they all would rather watch the French actress, if it were the correct thing to do, than listen to the opera.

At this point Anna enters, holding herself "very erect as usual and looking straight before her ... moving with the quick, firm, yet light step which distinguishes her from other society women." She has been to the Countess Lydia's; because she wants to be accepted here, she repeats a bit of scandal she has picked up in the other salon. It is not long, however, before she and Vronsky are sitting alone and apart. Their absorption in each other causes some comment. This is not surprising, but when Karenin is announced and the two still seem unaware of their aloofness Princess Betsy intervenes. Anna takes the hint and they separate. Even so, Anna does not join her husband, who is being somewhat pompous on the subject of military conscription. After remaining a half hour, Karenin seeks out his wife and suggests they go home together. Without really looking at him, she turns down his proposal by saying she wants to stay for supper. He returns home without her.

Time passes more slowly for Levin. Even with his busy life on his estate, he discovers that peace can be illusive.

Levin, conscious that it is not good for a young man to live alone, knows that it is impossible for any girl to take Kitty's place in his heart. Memories of her torment him. In the midst of one of those rare, beautiful springs, he holds to his resolution of living a pure life. Days had been harassing enough in February when, receiving a letter from Masha, he had gone to Moscow, seen his brother, paid his debts, lent him money and sent him off to a watering place abroad. In late winter he had also been occupied with his theory that not the soil, not the climate, and not scientific knowledge, but an understanding of the immutable character of the Russian peasant was the key to agrarian success. He was writing a book. After Lent came the thaws and then spring.

For Levin spring is the time for projects. He is full of them. He has ideas about the cattle. He must see the carpenter. He must put an end to slovenly farm work. The horses and stables need attention. The bailiff must be brought into line. He storms from one trouble spot to another.

On some lovely days, however, it is impossible to be angry. On such blessed days, he is in the best of spirits as he trots along on his good little cob. The farther he goes, the more plans he concocts. Plant trees here; dig a pond there; put a cattle yard beyond.

One morning he comes upon some laborers sitting by the edge of the road. Because the boss laborer has shirked his job, Levin is forced to correct him. The man answers back but Levin is slow to anger. "Please don't argue," he says, "but do as you are told."

Afterward, Levin mounts his horse again and continues his ride. The clover is coming up splendidly in the stubble field. Everything is capital. Annoyances are soon out of mind. On his return, as he approaches the house, he hears the tinkling of a bell. He suspects someone has come from the railway station. Who? He hopes it is some fine person to talk to. When he recognizes Oblonsky, he flings up his hands in joy.

"I've come," says the Prince, embracing Levin," one, to see you, two, to get some shooting, and three, to sell the Yergushovo forest."

The first two reasons please Levin but concerning the third, he is doubtful. He had known Oblonsky was being urged by his father-in-law to sell the forest in order to raise money, which was always in short supply. Nevertheless, he does not allow this to dampen their spirits. He looks forward to a shoot with Oblonsky, who is an excellent marksman and a first-rate hunting companion. They enjoy a good talk and a good dinner. Oblonsky, always kind and quick to understand, is especially flattering to Levin's old nurse and housekeeper. (He would rather have seen a pretty girl in an apron in charge.) He listens with interest to Levin's talk about his book, his estate plans, his management problems. Levin, taking advantage of the break in his long solitude, talks at great length. Both men avoid any reference to Kitty.

As the sun begins to sink behind the bare treetops of the forest, they get ready for their bird hunt. Oblonsky takes the canvas cover off his varnished gun case and puts together his expensive gun while Levin's servant, Kuzma, already sensing a generous tip, helps to put on his stockings and boots. Laska, Levin's dog, is excited; she knows where her master is going. The place is not far off, in a little aspen grove near a stream.

When they arrive, the men listen for the birds. Their eyes are fixed either upon the watchful Laska or upon the treetops above. Suddenly, Levin sees a bird against the dusky blue sky. Just as the bird's long beak and neck are distinctly visible, and he is taking aim, there is a flash from behind the bush where Oblonsky is standing. Another flash follows. The bird is seen beating its wings in an attempt to stay up. It stops, is stationary for a moment, then falls to the ground with a thud. Laska, wagging her tail, brings the dead bird to Levin. The sport is excellent. The shots ring out. Oblonsky gets another, then a pair. Levin is also successful.

Later Levin asks Stiva quite calmly about Kitty. Is she married yet? If not, when? Oblonsky tells Levin that Kitty has been very ill and has been taken abroad by her parents for her health's sake. When he continues the story of her disappointment over Vronsky, Levin is humiliated and then angry. It is insulting that Vronsky refused the girl who refused him. This puts him in a very dark mood, and so they return to the house where a Polish agent has come, by appointment with Oblonsky, to close the sale of the forest. Levin's depression deepens when he recognizes the agent as one whom he knows to be dishonest. He warns Oblonsky that he is being cheated. Oblonsky, already smelling as large sum of money, goes ahead with the deal in spite of his friend's disgust.

Levin launches into a tirade on the subject of the impoverishment of the nobility - the class of which he is a member. He says he is not worried about extravagances, nor about the peasants who acquire a little land now and then from an idler. He is concerned about the foreign speculators who buy up superb estates for half their value; for them he has nothing but wrathful condemnation. This brings him to the subject of the aristocracy.

"You consider Vronsky an aristocrat? I don't ... I consider people like me aristocrats, people who can point back to three or four honorable generations, all with the highest degree of breeding (talent and intelligence are a different matter) who have never curried favor with anyone ... so I prize what has come to me from my ancestors or been won by hard work ... we are the aristocrats."

Meanwhile Vronsky, in St. Petersburg, never thinks about Kitty. He is completely absorbed in his new passion. Everyone guesses, more or less correctly, about his relations with Madame Karenina. Most of the younger men in the regiment envy him for the one thing that is most troublesome to him, the exalted position of Karenin and the consequent publicity given the affair. The younger women, who had so long heard Anna's virtues being praised, are rejoicing at the mud they can now sling. The older people and highly-placed personages are annoyed at the impending scandal. Even Vronsky's mother, who had at first been pleased (because she believed that a liaison with a fashionable woman would add the finishing touch to a brilliant young man's education), changes her opinion when she learns that Vronsky is refusing important posts so that he can near Anna. She worries that this is not a passing fancy, but a passion that may lead to disaster. She has not seen him since his return to St. Petersburg.

CHAPTERS 20 THROUGH 27

Vronsky has a second interest that is nearly as compelling as his love for Anna. He is passionately fond of horses. He rides them, he owns them, he races them, even jockeys them. For this last, he trains and keeps his weight down by avoiding sweets and starchy foods. This year there is to be an officers' steeplechase. Vronsky has bought a thoroughbred English mare and entered the race. In spite of his affair with Anna, he is looking forward to the race with intense, if reserved, anticipation. He needs occupation and distraction, apart from his love, to refresh himself and find rest from the violent emotions, that agitate him.

The famous race course, not far from St. Petersburg at Krasnoe, is surrounded by summer villas of noble families, including the Karenin's. The regiment has set up temporary quarters there too. On the morning of the race, after eating his beefsteak, he goes to see his trainer and to inspect the mare. The horse is as nervous at the owner. The trainer wants to keep Vronsky out of the box but he insists. She is a marvelous beauty, and when Vronsky puts his face up to hers, the trainer senses the accord between them. On his way out Vronsky catches a glimpse of the new stallion his main rival is to ride. The trainer is most anxious for Vronsky to stay calm and urges him to do nothing to disturb himself.

When he returns to his quarters, his roommate hands him letters from his mother and brother. Vronsky, knowing that they contain further admonitions concerning his affair with Anna, sticks them, unopened, into his pocket. He is in no mood for the joshing hilarity of his officer friends who are looking forward to the day. The court will be at the races; the emperor, himself, is sure not to miss the event. Vronsky knows that the eyes of the important will be upon him. Karenin will feel he has to be there too. (Karenin has been abroad, but Vronsky knows he has just returned.)

In St. Petersburg, Karenin is having a busy morning. He started early, reading a complicated brochure, so that he would be prepared to impress the cultured foreigner who is being sent by the Countess Lydia Ivanovna. His secretary has made numerous other appointments for him. In between these, his doctor tells the secretary that something emotional must be disturbing him. Knowing glances are exchanged. Karenin sees his steward. He receives some money to take to Anna as her semi-monthly allowance. He will proceed to their summer villa after the races. He has not seen her or his son recently. He invites the secretary to go with him. He has taken to the habit of having a third person along when he sees Anna.

Meanwhile at Krasnoe, Vronsky orders his caleche, a low-wheel light carriage with a folding top. He tells his companions he has promised to see the horse-dealer, Bryansky; they suspect that seeing Bryansky means seeing someone else. This is indeed true. Vronsky orders the coachman to drive the five miles to Peterhof where Anna is living. In spite of delay in a thunderstorm, he still leaves the carriage some distance from the estate, as is his custom. He slips in through the garden, where he meets the gardener who informs him that Karenin is not yet there. He finds Anna on the terrace; she has come to await Seriohza whose walk must have been interrupted by the rain. Vronsky has begun to resent her son. He is the one, more than any other, who has interfered with his meetings with Anna. In front of the child, their conversations and actions are friendly but always formal. The boy loves his mother, but has sensed Vronsky's antipathy. He is puzzled. How can he possibly dislike someone whom his mother likes, and who obviously likes to be with her?

On this afternoon, Anna appears to be in a serious mood. She tries to hide her feelings by talking about the race. She is being called for by the Princess Betsy. It will be a gala occasion. Nevertheless, Vronsky is aware of her preoccupation. He dislikes the need to be secretive about their meetings. So does Anna. Why should they not be as open as so many of their friends are about their affairs? Vronsky wants to put an end to their false position. He wants Anna to leave her husband, to go away with him, to live abroad. She deliberately changes the subject as she has many times before; she does not want to discuss their position. Today, when he forces her to talk, she is hurt. Yet she knows there is more reason than ever to talk today. Upon his urging she at last tells him why. She is pregnant. Then, it is his turn not to want to talk. It is late and he must be off. Tenderly, he promises to return late that night.

In his confusion Vronsky tells the coachman to drive to Bryansky's. He stays only five minutes, getting back for the race just in time. He has barely changed his clothes when his mare is being led out. Once again he is amazed at her beauty. Frou-

Frou is as excited as he is. Just after he has mounted, Mahotin, riding the rival stallion rushes past. This excites Frou-Frou even more and Vronsky is very angry at Mahotin's discourtesy, which he believes was deliberate. There are thirteen entrants in the steeplechase, the third and chief event of the day. Vronsky draws number seven. The starter has trouble with the horses that are crowding each other. The spectators in the pavilions are eager. The Countess Lydia, Karenin, and Anna have raised their field glasses. One false start after another. Finally - they are Off!

Vronsky and the mare clear the ditches and the various barriers with room to spare. After a poor start, they are soon but a length behind Mahotin. When Vronsky thinks the time has come for the mare to close the gap, she has the idea split seconds before he does. "My beauty," he calls as she takes the lead. The last jump is still ahead. It is less difficult than some of the earlier ones and Vronsky thinks the race is his. Frou-Frou clears easily, and because he wants to win with an even bigger margin, he lets her go, practically on her own. As he relaxes for an instant, he makes a serious blunder. He shifts his position backward. Suddenly one of Frou-Frou's legs is going down. His own foot is trailing. The mare is on the ground. What has happened? Vronsky is unhurt. He almost wishes he were. Frou-Frou is in agony. Her back is broken. Vronsky's shift had broken it. The doctors run forward. The horse must be destroyed. Almost at once, Vronsky's closest friend is on the track. As quickly as he can, the officer leads Vronsky away. He does not really come to himself until he reaches home, a half-hour later.

CHAPTER 28 THROUGH 35

From the pavilion, Anna had watched the accident and Karenin had watched Anna. She groaned. When word came that the horse was dead, but the rider unhurt, she did not know whether to believe her ears. What Karenin saw on Anna's face he had really known for a long time, but had not allowed himself to believe. He went over to her and offered to take her home. She told him to leave her alone. Princess Betsy tried to save the situation by saying that, since she had brought Anna, she would take her home. When Karenin persists, Anna gives him her arm and they go home in a closed carriage.

Anna is hardly aware of his presence. Earlier that afternoon, when she had watched him walking about in the crowd of important personages, she had hated him. She saw him condescendingly acknowledging obsequious bows, then exchanging nonchalant greetings with his equals, then trying hard to catch the eye of some great one. She loathed him. "Nothing but ambition, nothing but a desire to get on - that is all there is to his soul," she thought, "and as for those lofty ideals of his, his passion for culture, religion, they are so many tools for advancement."

Sitting beside him in the carriage, she worries only about her lover. Karenin determines to rebuke her for the exhibition she has made. Instead, he says something about the cruel spectacle the steeplechases have become. Anna is contemptuous. While she is half-listening, he finally gets to the point and asks her for appearance's sake, not to behave as she has been. He expects her to tell him, as she had before, that his suspicions are ridiculous. But the expression on her face gives him little hope. "Possibly I am mistaken," he continues, "In that case, I beg your pardon."

Looking with despair into his cold face, she tells him, "I listen to you, but I am thinking of him. I love him, I am his mistress; I cannot endure you, I am afraid of you and I hate you…. You can do whatever you like with me."

His whole face assumes the solemn immobility of the dead during the remainder of the drive. When they reach the house, his voice shakes as he says, "I must insist that you conform outwardly to propriety until such time as I take measures to secure my honor and inform you of them." He alights first and helps her out. In the presence of the servants he presses her hand in silence, reseats himself in the carriage and drives back to St. Petersburg.

"Thank God, everything's over with him," cries Anna and immediately glances at her watch. How long to wait? She knows Vronsky is bound to come. Her blood is on fire.

Meanwhile, Prince Shcherbatsky, his wife and daughter are comfortably settled at a fashionable German watering place. The Princess is enjoying the foreigners of importance; an English Lord and a German Royal Princess are in residence. The Prince dislikes the strange ways and customs; he is ill at ease and insists on being his own true Russian self. Kitty is somewhat bored. Her only distraction is watching the people around her. She enjoys studying them and tries to guess their history and their motives. As is typical of her, she thinks only the best. Her attention is particularly attracted to the companion of an older, invalid Russian woman, Madame Stahl. Madame was once well known at court and Kitty's mother is somewhat chagrined that she has not taken the trouble to acknowledge the Shcherbatsky's presence. She agrees for Kitty's sake to make the first move; the Princess introduces herself to the companion, who is known as Varenka.

"Of Mademoiselle Varenka one would say not that she had passed her first youth, but that she was, as it were, someone without youth: she might be nineteen or she might be thirty." At any rate, Kitty is fascinated by her charm. She is constantly performing little services for this or that sick person. At one point she tactfully, if somewhat dramatically, saves Nicolai Levin, who is there with Masha, from an embarrassing situation. Nikolai had been berating a German doctor; he had been shouting noisily, disturbing everyone, when Varenka quietly led him away. The Scherbatskys were relieved because they had been avoiding Nikolai, whose appearance is extremely disagreeable. Kitty was even more relieved when Nikolai and the woman depart. The sight of them had inevitably brought to mind his brother and memories of their relationship.

Kitty is drawn more and more to Varenka. The two girls exchange confidences. Varenka had been in love herself until her young man's mother intervened and persuaded him to marry someone else. Varenka teaches Kitty that her soul will find peace if she does good deeds. Madame Stahl has found such peace. She has the reputation of being highly philanthropic and deeply religious. No one knows Madame Stahl's denomination- Catholic, Protestant, or Orthodox-but the highest dignitaries of all the churches know her. She gives Kitty a testament which Kitty reads each night. Each day Kitty embarks on altruistic campaigns. She finds her own mental distress disappearing.

Kitty takes particular pleasure in helping Petrov, a poor Russian artist who is sick. Even though there is little money, his wife and child are with him. At first Kitty had to struggle with the repugnance she felt for his consumptive condition. When she has overcome this aversion, she finds herself enjoying his company. She also enjoys secret chats with his wife about the invalid's progress and their schemes to draw him away from his work, and to get him outdoors. The man himself gazes at her in a touching way, making her conscious of her own goodness. Then, little by little, Kitty becomes aware that the wife is watching her when she is alone with Petrov having her portrait painted. When his wife sends her a note, saying that Petrov has decided to leave the spa (which is untrue), Kitty is completely confused. She gradually realizes that her altruism is not turning out so well. Doing good is fine for Varenka, who performs her services with charm and true selflessness, but for Kitty-she could not help doing good in other ways. She had to admit that she was pleased with the interest that even this poor sick man had shown in her.

At this point her father returns from a short side trip and blows a bit of fresh air over the complications. He has a few cynical comments to make about Madame Stahl and her pietism. He had known her husband before she divorced him. He shocks Kitty by saying that Madame does not get up because her legs are short and she has a very ugly figure. Sorry because of his daughter's disillusionment, he is kind when he sympathetically points out that it is better to do good so that no one knows you are doing it.

The trip abroad has been healthful in more than one way. Kitty returns to Russia, cured. "She was not so carefree and lighthearted as before, but she was at peace. The misery she had felt in Moscow had become only a memory to her."

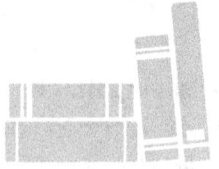

ANNA KARENINA

TEXTUAL ANALYSIS

PART THREE

....

CHAPTERS 1 THROUGH 8

When Sergei Ivanovich Koznyshev wants a rest from intellectual work, he goes to the country. Accordingly, at the end of May, he arrives at Levin's. The two brothers have very different views on country life; as a consequence, they often irritate each other in spite of a deep-rooted fondness. Koznyshev looks upon the country as a place to do as little as possible. If your body gets restless from lying in the sun, a little stupid fishing helps. If your mind feels rusty, it can be oiled by working out some new chess gambits. If you want more stimulation, you can talk or argue. This means talking to Levin.

To Levin country life means work in all four seasons. May and June are the busiest months, when every worker has much to accomplish before bad weather sets in again. It is irksome to Levin to take time out when he is needed in so many places at once. Besides, he is no match for Koznyshev in debate. For example, Koznyshev says he loves the peasants, and it is true that he can talk to them and enjoy their company without condescension. Levin, on the other hand, will never say that he loves the peasants. To him they are men just like all other men. There are good peasants and bad. He likes them when they are strong, gentle and fair, but he can get exasperated with their carelessness, drunkenness and lying.

Koznyshev wants Levin to try to take an interest in the Zemstvo again. He feels he has a duty to help set up schools, get better roads, originate schemes for midwives and medical care. Levin argues that many peasants will steal a new bridge, and that during most seasons of the year, doctors cannot get through the snow or mud. Consequently, the peasants should know how to take care of themselves. He has little faith in doctors anyway. At one point he goes so far as to say that he is not sure that a peasant who knows how to read is better off.

During these discussions, Levin realizes he wants to do something he had a taste of the year before, but hesitates because he knows Koznyshev is bound to disapprove. He wants to stand in line with peasants and mow for an entire day. He wants the exercise, even though the exertion is extreme. Early one morning, long before his brother is out of bed, he joins the peasants. After taking up a scythe and receiving instruction from a kindly, old mower named Titus, Levin gradually learns. In spite of the sweat that drenches his back, Levin feels very happy. Sometimes his line is smooth as Titus'. But as soon as he begins to think about what he is doing and how hard it is, he mows badly. It is breakfast time before he knows it. Later, in the heat of the day, it does not seem such hard work. There are moments of oblivion when his body swings the scythe in an almost automatic rhythm. These moments, completely devoid of thought, are happy ones.

All constraint between peasants and master disappears. At dinner time some of the young lads bathe in the stream, others untie their bundles and arrange places for an after-dinner rest. Titus shares his crumpled bread with Levin. Chatting with him about family affairs, Levin feels much closer to him than to his brother. When the old fellow says his prayer and lies down under a bush, Levin does the same and falls asleep at once. When he awakes and sees how much has been cut, he is amazed. The forty-two men have already cut the whole of the big meadow, a job that used to take thirty men two days in the time of serf labor. At teatime, when some sit down and light their pipes, Levin does not feel tired. He asks Titus whether they might even mow a certain hill before quitting. Titus answers with a question: "Would there be a drop of vodka for the lads?" At Levin's nod, there is a shout and they start to mow as if competing in a race.

When he gets back to the house, Koznyshev tells his brother that he has spent the day in the village; there he learned that peasants do not like the gentry to work with them. This information is not news to Levin and he is not dismayed. What is important is the record amount of mowing that has been done, and more important to him is his new friendship with a wonderful old man.

While Oblonsky went from Moscow to St. Petersburg on official business, and took advantage of the trip to enjoy the races at Krasnoe and the nearby villas of his acquaintances, Dolly and the children have moved to the country to cut down expenses. The estate, Yergushovno, had been part of her dowry. (The forest her husband had recently sold was part of it.) It is about thirty-five miles from Levin's. At first she finds country life difficult. Since it rains in the corridor and nursery, the children's beds have to be moved to the drawing room. There is no kitchen maid to be found. Most of the cows are calving so that there is not enough milk. It is impossible to get any fowls. There is no place to bathe - no proper cupboards - not even an ironing board. However, Dolly has her Matrona Filimonovna! The two women, without the help of the bailiff (whom Oblonsky had hired), set things to rights. Before long there is even time for the mother to enjoy her children. All six of them are charming in their different ways. Dolly loves them - even takes them to mass - after a great deal of fussing over their clothes. Lilly, the smallest, is bewitching when, after taking the sacrament, she says unexpectedly in English: "Please, some more."

CHAPTERS 9 THROUGH 16

One day, when Dolly is returning with her children from a nearby stream where they had gone to bathe, they meet Levin. He has ridden over to see them and to offer his help as Oblonsky had requested. As Levin looks at Dolly, he finds himself face to face with one of the pictures of the family life of his dreams. Running about with the children, sending their governess into peals of laughter with his broken English, and talking to Dolly about his rural affairs, he drops into the mood of childish lightheartedness that Dolly particularly likes in him. This prompts her to talk about Kitty.

He begs her not to discuss his proposal, but as he does so, he is conscious that hope still stirs in his heart. She explains that when Kitty refused him, she was seeing Vronsky frequently. Kitty was so young that her refusal at that moment proves nothing. Dolly is prevented from continuing, to Levin's relief, by her daughter Tanya, who has to be rebuked. After this scolding there is a scream from the nursery. Tanya has Grisha by the hair. As a result, Levin's idyllic picture of family life gets a new tint.

Later in the summer, when Levin goes to the village on business in connection with his sister's estate some fifteen miles away, he perceives something wrong about the division of the hay. He is convinced, partly because of the village elder's reluctance to talk, that he is being cheated. After a lengthy dispute, he insists that the owner's share be measured afresh. While this is being done, his attention is drawn to a rosycheeked peasant girl who is tossing hay into a wagon. A young lad is helping her. The pair seem so full of fun and happy. When Levin learns that they are already man and wife, he is envious of their healthy and youthful mirth. Their common work seems to make them happy.

Even though Levin has just been hard on the peasants who have tried to rob him, they are already losing all signs of rancor against him. Because of the short summer night, many of them spend it in the meadow instead of returning to their homes. Levin listens to their singing. One of the women, singing in a wild, untrained voice, carries the verses while half a hundred voices, some gruff, some soft, do the choruses. With the coming of the dawn, Levin is still wide awake because of too much thinking. "Take a wife." "Marry a peasant girl." "My ideas of family life are nonsense." "It's all much simpler ... and easier."

With his eyes fixed on the ground, he hears a jingle of bells in the distance. A four-in-hand carriage with luggage on top advances toward him. The driver is skillful and, as he lurches away from the ruts, Levin catches a glimpse of a young girl holding the ribbons of her cap in both hands. Serene thoughtful she is gazing at the sunrise. It is Kitty. A look of wonder and delight shows in her face as she recognizes him. He realizes she must be coming from the station on her way to Yergushovo.

"No," he says to himself, "however good the simple life of toil may be, I cannot. I love her."

On the night of his return to St. Petersburg after the races, Karenin dispatches a letter to Anna. He has had enough time to analyze his situation, and to think of what other men, as far back as Menelaus, have done when wronged by their wives. In modern Russia, some husbands demanded satisfaction in duels. He knows himself well enough to admit that he lacks that sort of physical courage; also, he knows his friends would not permit his dueling. If he were to be killed, Russia would lose too valuable an administrator. Divorce is another alternative. Would not his enemies take advantage of such a scandal? Another possibility is separation without divorce. That would merely allow Anna to continue her liaison. Certainly she should not be allowed that happiness. Rather, she should be punished. The affair with Vronsky must be terminated; she must join her husband again! He will forgive her. Yes, that is the Christian thing to do. His mind is made up. In this vein, he writes and takes care to enclose money for Anna's return trip.

The next morning at Peterhof, Anna rebukes herself for not having told Vronsky the night before what she had blurted out to her husband. Even so, she knows why she has not. She dreads the disgrace. Also she knows she is afraid. She is terrified that Karenin may take her son away from her. She decides to flee with the boy. She gives orders and packing begins.

At this point Karenin's letter arrives. She is amazed at this magnanimous Christianity. How upright! How clever he is! The world will never know how, for eight years, he has crushed everything that was living in her. She had striven to love him, but he had never seemed to sense that she was a woman who needed love. Her anger at the letter gives way to tears. She weeps because she knows her dream of having her situation cleared up has been destroyed. It takes all her strength to regain control. She realizes she must see Alexei (Vronsky). She orders the packing to stop. She hopes she may find him at Princess Betsy's.

CHAPTERS 17 THROUGH 32

Anna is disappointed not to find Vronsky at one of the Princess' social gatherings. The people there are at their cleverest; the chatter is both more meaningless and more brilliant than usual. There seems to be a double meaning in every remark. While Anna awaits an opportunity to leave, she has a bit of luck. She manages to get her hands on a note Betsy is sending to Vronsky to invite him to dinner. Secretly, Anna encloses a message of her own in Betsy's note. She asks Vronsky to meet her in the garden of a certain old lady, where she can pay a call without suspicion.

Vronsky receives the note from the Princess' footman while he is attending a banquet for a fellow officer who has received a promotion. There has been plenty to drink. Vronsky has recovered his spirits after a bad morning spent going over his finances. They are in a poor shape, since his mother has withdrawn her allowance because of Anna. He is now exhilarated, not just from the champagne, but also because his friend, the guest of honor, urged him to seek advancement. Russia, he said, needs men like Vronsky. He can never be bought either by money or by flavor. To stay in power he never has to invent policy. Because of this he is free from the temptations that beset lesser men.

Anna's urgent desire to see him flatters him even more. He is a very contented young man as he sets out in a hired carriage to keep his rendezvous with her. As soon as he sees her, however, he knows something has happened and that their meeting will not be a happy one. She tells Vronsky once that she has told her husband of her love for him. She watches his eyes for his first reaction and misunderstands what she sees, because Vronsky's mind jumped to the immediacy of a duel. However, he won't admit that this was his first thought. He does not want to frighten her. As a consequence, his words, when he says how glad he is that the need for secrecy is gone, have an empty ring. When he leads her into the shadow of the garden as someone unexpectedly passes, she realizes how long it will be before their state can change. He feels very sorry for her and, for the first time in his life, he is on the point of weeping.

When Anna deliberately talks to her husband the next day, she is completely rebuffed. Karenin says that he will ignore her affair so long as the world knows nothing of it, and so long as his name is not disgraced. In return for such magnanimity, she will continue to enjoy the privileges of being his wife without fulfilling the duties.

As the summer progresses in the country, Levin tries to keep Kitty out of his thoughts. Her refusal has erected too many fences. He feels he cannot ask her to marry him now, simply because she cannot be the wife of the man she wanted to marry. He decides, instead, to visit a neighbor in the opposite direction. Nikolai Ivanovich Sviazhsky is an old friend and shooting companion. On his way over, Levin stops at a well-kept, efficient farm. He is jealous that his estate is very poorly managed by comparison. The difference is that the prosperous peasant's farm is a family project where they see to everything themselves. They are not dependent on hired labor. At Sviazhsky's the conditions are no better than at Levin's. Sviazhsky is clever and highly cultivated, also sensible and kind-hearted. Yet Levin invariably fails to understand him when he tries to penetrate below the surface. The man seems to be afraid that Levin may see him as something other than the self-satisfied, good-humored man he wants to appear. Levin enjoys the old-fashioned, hard-headed, obstinate talk of some of Sviazhsky's neighbors who come to grumble that "land which with serf-labor and good management used to yield nine-fold now in the half-crop system (half to the owner, half to the peasant) yields threefold. Emancipation of the peasants has been the ruin of Russia." This sort of talk makes Levin itch to get back to work on his book. His thesis is that the fancy theories of European agrarians and economists, including the Englishman Mill, are not transferable to Russia unless one understands the uniqueness of the Russian peasant. Levin flees rather suddenly and rudely. His haste is also caused by the sight of the low-cut bodice of Sviazhsky's sister-in-law. This is too frightening for a bachelor so sensitive about his eligibility.

On his return home, he throws himself with renewed vigor into his own reform schemes. He tries to put into effect a plan to offer land to the peasants on very generous terms. He is distrusted for the most part, but because one or two go along, he persists. More bungling on the part of his probable proteges throws him into despair.

The arrival of his brother Nikolai helps little. When Nikolai unwinds his scarf and smiles with unnaturally glittering eyes, Levin knows that Nikolai's enthusiasm for a new life is hollow. "Myakov has promised me a post ... you know I got rid of that woman ... I want to turn over a new leaf." Levin sees nothing but death when he looks at his brother. With irresistible force he feels it in himself too. Nikolai once enjoyed as strong and healthy a body as his own. Levin sees death, or the advance of death, everywhere. Everything becomes dark; he feels that there is but one hope to clutch to-his work. This he clings to tenaciously.

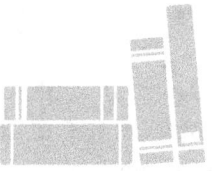

ANNA KARENINA

TEXTUAL ANALYSIS

PART FOR

....

CHAPTERS 1 THROUGH 12

The Karenins, husband and wife, continue to live in the same house, but they are totally estranged. Though Vronsky never comes to the house, Anna meets him away from home and her husband is aware of it. However, there comes a time when the rule is broken.

Vronsky has been very busy acting as official guide and chief entertainer for a foreign prince who is fond of extravagant all night carousals. Vronsky, seeing in this prince a likeness of his former self, is disgusted and bored. This causes him to resent the time he has been away from Anna.

So does she. They both looked forward to the end of this period, but Anna is unfortunately sick and cannot leave the house. Unwisely they arrange a meeting at home. As Vronsky is about to go up the steps to the house, he sees the Karenin carriage. Impetuously, because he is late, Vronsky goes up and meets Karenin himself in the hall. Nevertheless, Karenin leaves.

Anna and Vronsky have an unhappy time, and the next morning Karenin informs Anna of his intention to leave Moscow, send the boy to a relative, and proceed with a divorce. Anna becomes hysterical and begs Karenin not to take the boy away. He is adamant. Anna fears that death will take her in childbirth; she tells Vronsky she almost wishes it. Vronsky cannot understand Karenin; according to aristocratic tradition, the matter should have been settled by a duel. This is the code Vronsky has always lived by. Since the code no longer fits his way of life, he finds himself ineffectual and confused; chances for advancement come and go. His whole life is devoted to Anna. He no longer shares officer's quarters. Living alone, he begins to resent the things which have changed him. He recognizes that Karenin's actions have wrought changes in Anna too.

She has lost much of her vivacity. Fearing the probable loss of her son, she has wanted to spend more and more time with him instead of going about in society with Vronsky. Her health is poor. And now, of course, she is very pregnant and morose.

Moscow, where Karenin had to go on business, is a bustling metropolis. On his arrival, he meets Oblonsky, who invites him to dinner. Karenin begs off, explaining that he is very much involved in a government matter concerning the provinces. This is much too complicated for Stiva to understand; he keeps insisting. Finally Karenin tells him that he cannot accept his hospitality because he is divorcing his sister. Oblonsky, who cannot bring himself to believe Karenin's story implores him to come to dinner where he can talk to Dolly. Dolly will listen and understand, and her advice, he promises, will be worth considering. Karenin, in the end, agrees to come to dinner.

Because there is little that Oblonsky would rather do than entertain at small exclusive dinner parties, he takes great pains with the menu and the wines. Because there is still some cash left from the sale of the forest, he prepares an elaborate meal. The guest list is just as meticulously planned. To balance Karenin as a St. Petersburg man of affairs, Moscow's brilliant philosopher-Levin's brother, Koznyshev-is invited. As a counterpart to the earthy, but elderly Prince Shcherbatsky, Oblonsky selects the man about town, Turovtsyn, who could be counted on to produce a laugh should the intellectuals become stuffy. Besides these and a few others, Stiva takes delight in pairing Levin, who has just come to town, with Kitty.

At the dinner party these two can scarcely keep their eyes off each other. They take little part in the general conversation, even when it turns to the education of women. Here Karenin's cleverness seems to hide a sour note. Oblonsky is relieved, for the sake of his other guests, when Dolly leads Karenin off to the schoolroom for a private talk about Anna. Dolly is shocked when Karenin explains that he is not mistaken, because Anna herself has told him of her affair with Vronsky. Dolly is very sorry; she begs Karenin to take pity on Anna, who will be lost. In an effort to wring a promise from Karenin to forgive Anna, Dolly tells him about Oblonsky's betrayal. "In my anger and jealousy I wanted to throw up everything ... but I came to my senses ... the children are growing up ... my husband is coming back ... I have forgiven and you ought to forgive."

To this, Karenin answers that he hates Anna for all the wrongs she has done him. As he departs, his final remark is, "Love them that hate you! But you can't love those you hate."

CHAPTERS 13 THROUGH 23

When, after the dinner, Kitty and Levin find themselves alone and seated at a green-covered card table, they begin writing to each other with a piece of chalk. The discover that their thoughts are so similar that the first letters of works are all that is necessary for complete understanding. When he writes, "I, H, N, T, F, A, F, I, H, N, C, T, L, Y," she knows that he means, "I have nothing to forget and forgive I have never ceased to love you." They are dazed with happiness. When he sees in her eyes all he needs to know, and starts to write down just three letters, she answers "Yes" before he is finished!

At this point in the evening, Kitty is whisked off to the theatre by her father. Levin is at a complete loss as to how to spend the next fourteen hours before he can call at the Shcherbatsky's and formally ask the Prince for his daughter's hand. For want of something better to do, he asks his brother whether he can go to a meeting with him. Koznyshev is surprised and delighted. Levin finds the meeting pleasant, although the topic under discussion does not really interest him. Later at the hotel, he is pleased to discover that Yegor, the night man on duty, loved his wife when he married her. Alone in his room he is oppressively hot, so he opens the window and finds the air invigorating. The snow scene, which includes a cross silhouetted in front of the stars, is very peaceful and full of meaning for him. At six o'clock he hears bells ringing in the servant's quarters and suddenly realizes he is cold. From then on until noon, when he feels he can at last set out for Shcherbatsky's, he wanders the streets, seeing things he never saw before-all of which are extraordinary and interesting.

As expected, the Prince is very happy with Kitty's decision. He kisses her several times and then kisses his wife. In the confusion the two old people do not quite know whether it is they who are in love again or only their daughter. After receiving a round of congratulations from the rest of the household, Levin leaves. The next few days are wonderfully happy ones. When Kitty asks him to forget and forgive her first refusal of him, he says he also has something for her to forgive and forget. He wants no secrets between them, so he tells her that he is an agnostic and that he, at his age is no longer chaste. With her father's consent. Levin brings her his diary so she will know the worst. It shocks her even more than he had suspected. "It's awful, awful!" she cries. Nevertheless, she forgives him. From that time on, he considers himself unworthy of her more than ever, and prizes his undeserved happiness still more highly.

After his chat with Dolly, Karenin returns to his hotel where two telegrams await him. The first contains the news that another man has received an appointment Karenin coveted for himself. He is annoyed, not so much at having missed the post, but at having been so conspicuously passed over. The second is from Anna. "I am dying. I beg, I implore you to come. I shall die easier with your forgiveness."

He immediately suspects a trick. Then he recalls her confinement. There is the possibility that in a moment of agony, near death, she is penitent. He cannot cruelly ignore her. Accordingly, he reverses his plans, and sets out for St. Petersburg. When he arrives and hears that Anna was safely delivered the day before, he turns pale and at once realizes how intensely he had desired her death. He rushes up the stairs and finds Vronsky weeping in the little boudoir outside her bedroom. Making an effort, Vronsky gets up and says, "She is dying. The doctors say there is no hope. I am entirely in your hands, only let me be here."

Although Anna is frequently delirious, she can sometimes collect her thoughts. Gazing at Karenin with more tenderness and affection than he had ever seen in her eyes before, she begins, "Don't be surprised at me. I am still the same. But there is another woman in me. I'm afraid of her. It was she who fell in love with that man ... now I'm myself ... I only want one thing-for you to forgive me ... No, you can't forgive me! ... No, no, go away, you're too good."

Karenin's emotions reach a point where he gives up struggling against them. A glad feeling of love and forgiveness fills his heart. He kneels down, laying his head in the curve of her arm, which burns like fire, he sobs like a child. She becomes delirious again and the doctor had to intervene. A little later in another lucid moment, she tells Karenin to draw Vronsky's hands away from his face. "Give him your hand. Forgive him." The next instant she is screaming for morphia.

When the end is expected at any time, Vronsky goes home and tries to kill himself. Putting the revolver to the left side of his chest, with a powerful jerk of his whole hand, he pulls the trigger. When he finds himself on the floor and realizes that he is still alive, he fumbles for the revolver, but collapses before he can reach it. For several days he lies between life and death but three doctors and Varya, his brother's wife, manage to save him.

For the first time in Karenin's life he finds peace. The problems that had appeared insoluble, so long as he indulged in censure, recriminations and hatred, become simple and clear when he forgives and loves. He forgives Vronsky. He pities his son, in whom he had lost interest because of Anna. He pities the newborn little girl who is not his own child. As Anna slowly recovers, she sees the change that has come over her husband. At first she tries to focus on his nobility of character. However, as she recovers her health, she finds that he is still physically repulsive to her. His bossy ways, his affection for the new baby, his very kindness begin to annoy her. The differences between him and Vronsky are continually presenting themselves to her.

When she learns that Vronsky tried to commit suicide on her account, she knows she still loves him. Nevertheless, she refuses to see him, even though the Princess Betsy obtained Karenin's consent for Vronsky to have a farewell visit. He is leaving for Tashkent, where he has been appointed to a very important post.

At this juncture, fate seems to intervene in the person of Oblonsky. Stiva has been acute enough to sense that the passion between Anna and Vronsky is not a passing affair. Her illness and his attempted suicide have changed nothing. He knows neither of them will be happy without the other. He also is aware of Karenin's new spirit of love and forgiveness. Accordingly, he seeks out Karenin, plays on his feelings and persuades him to give up Anna. Karenin even consents to a divorce which will grant her custody of their son.

When Oblonsky tells the Princess Betsy that Karenin has agreed to a divorce, she passes the word to Vronsky. Almost immediately, Vronsky, without thinking twice about his new appointment, rushes to Anna and covers her with kisses. But Anna, who has not yet completely recovered, begins to tremble. She puzzles Vronsky when, with tears in her eyes, she declares she cannot accept Karenin's generosity now. She does not want a divorce anymore. Nevertheless, Vronsky is not so easily put aside. A month later Karenin is left alone in the house with his son, and Anna, still resolutely refusing a divorce, leaves with Vronsky for Italy.

ANNA KARENINA

TEXTUAL ANALYSIS

PART FIVE

....

CHAPTERS 1 THROUGH 16

For the six weeks prior to the wedding, Levin continues in the same state of delirious happiness. He has to reflect seriously upon only one thing. Oblonsky tells him that he cannot be married without a certificate stating that he has been to confession. Since he has not been to communion in nine years, he has not given a thought to the rules of the church. The idea of going to confession now oppresses him as an act of hypocrisy. Upon Oblonsky's insistence, Levin tries, without success to recapture the religious ardor he had experienced as a boy of sixteen. He cannot believe, yet at the same time he has no conviction that the teachings of the church are untrue. Therefore, in spite of an inner voice that tells him he is being deceitful, he goes through the steps preparatory to confession.

Finally, he is confronted by the priest, "a little old man with a scanty, grizzled beard and kind weary eyes," who reminds him that Christ is standing invisible before him. The priest asks whether Constantine Levin believes; when Levin says he has doubted, the priest explains that to doubt is a natural human weakness. He then asks Levin what special sins he has. Levin repeats that his chief sin is doubt. The priest replies, "What doubt can there be of the existence of God? Who adorned the celestial vault with the stars? Who decked the earth with her beauty? ... You are about to enter into holy matrimony. ... What sort of upbringing can you give your little ones ... your innocent babes when they ask ... will you reply, 'I don't know'?" When Levin remains silent, the priest pronounces the absolution and lets him go. Levin has a feeling of relief that he has come through it without lying.

Concerning the wedding ceremony itself, the Princess and Dolly insist that all the **conventions** be observed. For one thing, Levin is not to see Kitty on the day of the wedding. However, in the afternoon, after a bachelor dinner, Levin is assailed with doubts. Could he possibly be worthy of her? Does the poor girl know what she is doing? Feeling that he must give her a last chance to back out, he rushes over to her house where he finds her, with a maid, sorting old dresses to give away. Needless to say, Kitty tells him she loves him because she understands him so perfectly, and because she knows that everything he likes is good. The Princess discovers the pair together, and half-humorously and half in earnest, she sends him home to dress.

The church is lighted for the wedding. The crowd presses round the windows and peeps through the gratings. Inside, the wrought gold of the icons glitters before the candles. The church is flooded with light. To one side, whispered conversations are going on among the swallow-tails, the white ties, the uniforms, the brocades, and the velvets and satins. But where is the bridegroom? The bride is waiting to be told he has arrived at the church. The delay is awkward. Finally, Oblonsky arrives with the explanation. Levin had packed and sent away his last clean shirt. Kuzma was sent out to get one.

"Can it really be true?" Levin asks himself in the middle of the ceremony. He steals a glimpse at the bride's quivering lips and watches her little, white-gloved hand shake as it holds the candle. Several times the bridal pair try to guess what they are to do next and blunder. The same priest who confessed Levin corrects them. By the time God's two servants, Constantine and Ekaterina, plight their troth and the final "amen" floats through the air, a lump rises in Constantine's throat and unruly tears come to his eyes.

Vronsky and Anna, after traveling for three months and visiting Venice, Rome and Naples, arrive at a small Italian town where they intend to stay for some time. Anna, during this period of freedom and rapid return to health, feels happy and full of life. The thought of Karenin's misery does not poison her. She is conscious of no disgrace. Separation from the son she loves does not cause her pain because the sweet baby girl, "his" child fills his place. The more she gets to know Vronsky, the more she loves him. To have him entirely to herself is a continual joy. He, ordinarily a virile man, never opposes her and seems to have no will of his own. But sometimes he is bored with inactivity; sight-seeing is not important enough for him. He clutches first at politics, then at new books, then pictures. In his youth, when he had not known what to do with his money, he had collected engravings. Now he settles down to painting in an effort to satisfy his undefined longings that demand gratification. He begins a portrait of Anna in an Italian costume.

There are two other Russians of interest in the village. One, Golenischev, is an ineffective intellectual who has been on the verge of writing a book for a long time, but is still collecting material. He introduces Vronsky and Anna to a Russian painter of some repute in his homeland. Golenischev says Mihailov is a queer modern, a freethinker reared in atheism, nihilism and materialism. He accuses the painter of being just another savage who sees negation in everything, one who says, "There is nothing else - evolution, natural selection, the struggle for existence - and that's all."

Nevertheless, Vronsky and Anna visit Mihailov's studio. They recognize his talent. Anna agrees, although Vronsky is painting her portrait, that Mihailov can do one too. After the fifth sitting, Vronsky is impressed with Mihailov's ability to capture Anna's peculiar beauty. Though it is only through this portrait that Vronsky himself learns this sweetest expression of her soul, it seems to him that he has always known it. While he is painting, Mihailov, in spite of his admiration for Anna, keeps his distance. He is glad when the portrait is finished. He no longer has to listen to Golenischev's disquisitions on art, and he no longer has to worry about what to say concerning Vronsky's painting. Every dilettante, even a count, has a right to paint what he wants, but this is distasteful to Mihailov.

Vronsky's interest in painting does not last long. With nothing to occupy him, he becomes bored again. The palazzo they have rented seems uncomfortable; every crack is an eyesore. They soon decide to go to Russia, to the country where Vronsky has a large estate. He will make arrangements with his brother about the division of their property, and Anna plans to see her son.

After three month's of marriage, Levin is still happy, but not at all in the way he had expected. He is continually forgetting that a wife needs occupation too. Her fussing about tablecloths, furniture, spare-room mattresses, and other petty worries jars him. Even though he knows that these cares are essential for her, the two quarrel. Fortunately disenchantment affords new enchantment, but does not always prevent unexpected collisions over trivialities.

One such disagreement follows the opening of a letter from Masha who had gone back to live with Nikolai. Nikolai had taken her to a provincial town where he had a government post, but he had quarreled with his chief and was on his way back when he was taken so ill. She doubted he would ever leave his bed. Levin decides to set out the next day and Kitty asks to go along. He reproaches her for such an idea, and suspects she wants to go because it would be dull to be left alone. He does not admit this stupid thought, but points out how bad the inns will be and what a hindrance she will be to his travel. He still cannot believe how much she loves him and wants always to be with him. Finally, amid tears and kisses, she convinces him and they leave together.

CHAPTERS 17 THROUGH 33

Levin's two fears - that his wife would not be up to travel, and that she would not be able to countenance a woman like Masha - are both groundless. When they arrive at the pretentiously modern, but conspicuously dirty inn, Kitty shows her true colors. In the first place she takes no offense at Masha. In addition, pity for Nikolai does not freeze her into horror, as it does her husband. She immediately sees the need for action. She sends for the doctor, and with Masha's help, they sweep and clean the room thoroughly. She gives orders with such gentle insistence that they are always obeyed. The sick man, washed and combed, lying between clean sheets and propped up on high pillows, has a new expression of hope on his face as he gazes steadily at Kitty. That she knows how to deal with death without fear is wonderful proof to Levin that she instinctively understands death. But Levin, who has thought and talked about death, fears it and feels at a loss. Since their conversation about religion during their engagement, neither has started a discussion on the subject. "But she regularly went to church, said her prayers and so on, always with the unvarying conviction that it was the necessary thing to do. In spite of this assertion to the contrary, she was firmly persuaded that he was as much a Christian as herself and indeed a far better one."

Kitty arranges for the administration of the sacrament and extreme unction to the sick man. With his large eyes fastened upon the icon which is set out on a card table, Nikolai prays fervently during the ceremony. After the anointing, he suddenly feels better and does not cough once in the course of an hour. He falls asleep, but when he wakes up and finds himself alone with Levin, he asks for the iodine bottle so that he may inhale the vapors. In a hoarse whisper he tells Levin that he "went through that farce for her sake. She is so sweet; but you and I can't deceive ourselves. This is what I pin my faith to." He begins to breathe over the bottle, as he squeezes it in his bony hand.

For several days the dying man lingers. One day Kitty herself has to remain in bed after a spell of nausea. On this day no one can soothe him. Only opium enables him to forget the incessant pain. His sufferings make him long for death; he begins to look on death as a fulfillment of his desire, as a happiness. When he can no longer lift his hands, Kitty sends for a priest to read the prayers for the dying. During the prayers, Nikolai shows no sign of life and the priest, touching the cold, bloodless hand, says that he is gone. But suddenly there is a faint stir in the clammy mustaches of the dying man; from the depths of his chest come the distinct words, "Not quite ... Soon." He smiles and then-is gone.

More than ever Levin is incapable of apprehending the meaning of death, but thanks to his wife's presence, he is not reduced to despair. In spite of death, he feels the need of life and love. Another equally unfathomable mystery presents itself. Kitty's indisposition is due to a new life stirring within her.

Meanwhile, Karenin finds himself alone and unwanted, put to shame, a laughing stock. He tries to find relief by interesting himself in Seriozha's education. He reads the newest books on education and **didactics** and engages a new tutor. Seriozha seems to improve but other personal matters do not. Finally, the Princess Lydia Ivanovna manages to insinuate herself and begins to direct his affairs. She is a member of a new mystical Christian cult that is spreading in St. Petersburg. She assures Karenin that God will support him; since God was in his heart when he let Anna go away, it was He who forgave and so Karenin cannot feel ashamed. Karenin, under this influence, believes that he is in possession of the most perfect faith and that his soul is free from sin. He is experiencing complete salvation here on earth. It is necessary for him to think, in his humiliation, that there is some height, however imaginary, from which he can look down.

During the period of this beautiful friendship with Karenin, the Countess Ivanovna, who has always been in love with someone-princess, princesses, doctors, journalists, slavophiles - now feels that she is genuinely in love for the first time. Then Anna returns to St. Petersburg. She writes to the Countess, begging her to arrange for her to see her son, Seriozha. Karenin is told of the letter and feels he cannot refuse Anna's request, but the countess thinks otherwise. She reminds Karenin that she has told Seriozha that his mother is dead and that he prays for God to have mercy on her soul. She insists that they have no right to inflict further torture on the child. As a result, she writes Anna:

"Madame, to remind your son of you might lead to questions on his part which it would be impossible to answer without implanting in the child's soul a spirit of condemnation towards what should be sacred for him; and in the circumstances I beg you to interpret your husband's refusal in the spirit of Christian love. I pray to Almighty God to have mercy on you. Countess Lydia."

One of Seriozha's favorite occupations is to keep a lookout for his mother during his walks. He does not believe in death generally; and when he accidentally learns from his old nurse that his mother is not dead, he watches every graceful and comely woman he sees in the street. One day, his father interrupts his musings for his Bible lesson. Karenin is very stern with his son. Seriozha is frightened that he will be punished, even though the next day is his birthday.

Anna also remembers the child's birthday. The more her fury at the Countess Ivanovna continues to increase, the more she is determined to see the child. She rushes to the toy store, and makes plans to go to the house early the next morning. She plans to bribe the hall porter, who will still be half asleep, and rush up to the nursery where Karenin is certain not to make an appearance before nine

When she arrives in the morning, the totally unaltered appearance of the house, which had been hers for nine years, affects here powerfully. As sweet and painful memories come back to her, she forgets where she is for the moment and cannot speak. With an imploring look at the old porter who recognizes her, she runs upstairs. At the door Anna hears the sound of a childish yawn. Seriozha is sitting up in bed, stretching and finishing a yawn. "Seriozha!" she whispers, walking softly up to the bed. He has grown taller and is thinner. He smiles with eyelids still half-closed. Suddenly he topples forward into her arms.

"I knew," he says. "Today is my birthday! I knew you'd come. I'll get up now ... Why are you crying mama?" He showers her with kisses.

In the meantime a great commotion is going in the servants' quarters. They all know the mistress has come. A meeting between her and the master is unthinkable. How is it to be prevented?

Upstairs, Anna is unable to speak. She does not know what to say to the boy, but Seriozha understands all she wants to say. He understands that she is unhappy and that she loves him. He clings to her in silence and whispers, "Don't go away. He won't come just yet."

But he does. After a swift glance in which she takes in Karenin's whole figure, she is seized with a fit of loathing and hatred for him. She pulls down her veil in disgust and almost runs out of the room. She has not had time to undo the parcel of toys, so she takes it back with her.

When she returns to her apartment at the hotel, the nurse brings in the chubby baby whose toothless smile invites a kiss. Anna takes her in her arms and dances about with her, but she is suddenly aware that her love for this sweet baby girl will never be as intense as her feeling for Seriozha. On him, the child of a man she did not love, she had concentrated all the love that had never found satisfaction.

Realizing this, her thoughts turn to Vronsky. She feels an unexpected love for him. Where is he? Why does he leave her alone? All at once a strange idea crosses her mind: what if he has ceased to love her? As though she wants to test him she decides to go out to the theater, sit in a box, and show herself to society, Vronsky begs her to give up the idea. He had hoped that the world would progress from its old-fashioned notions, but he had recently learned from his family and friends that he was acceptable in St. Petersburg, but Anna was not. He had not told her this, but she realized it in subtle ways. Even her old friend, the Princess Betsy, had called and stayed for only ten minutes, as though her courage had run out.

Obstinately Anna goes to the theater and is brutally snubbed. Vronsky and his family watch from the stalls, as the fashionable people in the adjoining box move out conspicuously. Back at the hotel, Anna cries at him in despair and anger, "It's all your fault, all your fault."

"But I begged you, I implored you not to go. I knew it would be unpleasant ..."

"Unpleasant!" she cries. "It was asful! As long as I live ..."

Vronsky is sorry for her, but in his heart he reproaches her. Drinking in the assurances of love that are so trite he is almost ashamed to utter them, she gradually grows calmer. The next day, they leave for the country.

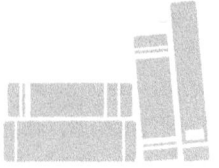

ANNA KARENINA

TEXTUAL ANALYSIS

PART SIX

CHAPTERS 1 THROUGH 16

Dolly, her children, their governess and the old princess are spending the first summer after Kitty's marriage at Pokrovskoe, Levin's estate. Other visitors include Varenka, Kitty's friend, and Sergei Ivanovich Koznyshev, Levin's half-brother. Kitty, who conducts her household affairs with unfailing care, has no little trouble getting enough fowl for all these people to eat. Levin likes the idea of having the rooms filled with many voices, but is constantly afraid that one of the children will bump into Kitty. Her mother refers to her pregnancy as an "interesting" condition. At the same time, he is not giving as much attention to the work of the estate as he had the summer before.

Varenka and Koznyshev seem to have fallen in love. Kitty is certain that Koznyshev will propose to Varenka; she recognizes signs of a blushing affection in her friend. Levin-who knows of his brother's love years ago for a girl who is now dead, and of his complete devotion to the intellectual life-watches the growing romance with skepticism. The old princess remarks that proposals are settled "by looks and smiles."

One afternoon when everyone goes to the woods to pick mushrooms, Varenka and Koznyshev find that their joy in being near each other increases continually. It should be easy for them to say what is filling their hearts. But against her will, and as if by accident, Varenka says, "So you did not find any? But, of course, there are always fewer in the middle of the road."

Koznyshev is vexed that she speaks about mushrooms, but for some reason, instead of the declaration that is on his lips, a perverse reflection causes him to ask, "What is the difference between a white boletus and a birch mushroom?"

Varenka trembles as she answers. As soon as she has spoken, both he and she understand that what was to have been said is now never going to be unsaid. Their excitation, which had reached its **climax**, begins to subside. Their plans had not come off. On the return trip Levin and Kitty read this in their crestfallen faces. However, the man and wife are too absorbed in their own love to worry about other romances.

The monotony of the summer is broken a second time with the arrival of Oblonsky and a handsome stout young man, a distant cousin of the Shcherbatskys. This dashing young ornament of St. Petersburg society, Vasenka Veslovsky, is introduced by Stiva as a "capital fellow and a keen sportsman."

From the very outset, it is obvious that this affable guest considers his visit in the country a piece of good fortune for both himself and the others. The women in particular respond to his cheerfulness with smiles. Levin, however, considers him a superfluous person and can hardly control himself when he overhears Kitty and Agatha Mihalovna deciding on what wines to serve this silly boy. It is nevertheless interesting that Vasenka has been to visit Anna and Vronsky at their estate not more than fifty miles away. Oblonsky suggests to Dolly that she visit his sister. When Dolly agrees, he turns to Kitty.

"I? Why should I go?" Kitty answers flushing deeply and glancing at her husband.

"Do you know Anna Arkadyevna, then?" Veslovsky asks her. "She's a very fascinating woman."

"Yes," she answers Veslovsky as she crimsons still more. Then going over to her own husband, she asks, "You are off shooting to-morrow?"

The flush that suffuses her cheeks when she talks to the young man arouses Levin's jealousy. Believing she has already been infatuated by the newcomer, he misinterprets her remark to mean, "Don't take him away from me." Vasenka, totally unaware of the misery his presence is causing, continues to watch Kitty with an affectionate smile in his eyes. Levin boils with rage, "How dare he look at my wife like that!"

The three men go off the next day on a bird-hunting trip. As they start out, Levin is amused by the lad's constant chatter, his witty stories and jokes. He is not amused when Vasenka carelessly lets his gun go off, nearly causing an accident. Soon after this **episode**, Vasenka reluctantly admits that he is missing his cigars and his pocketbook; he doesn't know whether he has lost them or left them behind. Since there are nearly four hundred rubles in the wallet, there is little else to do but go back to find out. Vasenka is willing to return, but Levin (thinking of Kitty) sends back the coachman. Levin does the driving until they stop for some shooting. He and Oblonsky try their luck while Vasenka is left to mind the horses. After a shot that he knows was off the mark, Levin turns at the sound of splashing growing louder and louder. Vasenka, in his eagerness to watch the shooting, has driven off the road and into the marsh. The horses are stuck in the mud.

Later, Oblonsky gets one duck. Levin is not so lucky. He makes a bad start and, invariably when this happens, he shoots badly for the rest of the day. He is jealous of Oblonsky who he hears calling, "Fetch it!" after almost every report. When he finally joins Oblonsky, he has five birds to Oblonsky's fourteen. They continue to the peasant's hut where they always put up and find Veslovsky already there. After cleaning up and eating, the three go to the newly swept hay barn where the coachman had made up special beds for them. Not one is sleepy. In spite of the day's exertions, they are talkative. Levin inevitably swings the topic to the subject of labor, honest and dishonest. He is against the railways and banking houses who afford the means of acquiring wealth without work.

"Why should we spend our time eating, drinking, shooting, doing nothing, while the peasant is at work from morning to night." asks Vasenka quite sincerely, the thought occurring to him for the first time in his life.

They are still talking when a peasant, expecting all to be asleep, comes to the barn for a crook. He explains they plan to take the horses to grass during the night. At this point, Veslovsky, straining his ears, asks the peasant if he doesn't hear women's voices singing. On learning that the maidservants are close-by, the young man joins them. Deciding to go also, Oblonsky teases Levin by reminding him that his honeymoon is over. "A man must be independent-have his own masculine interests. A man has to be manly."

"What does that mean? Running after servant girls?" asks Levin.

"Why not, if it amuses him? ... The main thing is to respect the sanctity of the home. Nothing of that kind at home." He is interrupted by Vasenka, who calls out that he has found a perfect Gretchen. Charmante. Oblonsky then puts on his slippers, lights a cigar and leaves Levin in the barn.

Levin gets up at dawn. His companions are deep in their first sleep when he crawls out. Laska, the dog, trots alongside her master. She is soon aware that mingled with the smells of roots and marsh grass is the scent of birds. One of these rises with guttural cry. Levin's shot catches it. By ten o'clock he has tramped twenty miles, and has nineteen birds and one duck to show Oblonsky. That Oblonsky is envious pleases him even more. All three are in a contented mood as they begin their homeward journey. Veslovsky sings songs and recalls with gusto his evening with the peasants; he has thoroughly enjoyed the outing. Levin admits he has too, and is particularly happy that he has overcome his animosity toward the friendly young man.

The next morning Vasenka tells Kitty how splendid the shooting had been. "What a pity it is that ladies are cut off from these delights!"

"Well, I suppose he must say something to the lady of the house," Levin tells himself, again fancying he detects something more than a smile in Vasenka's expression. Levin keeps casting glances at him; Kitty is flushed. Is she disturbed or pleased by the boy? Certainly she knows the effect her chatting is having on her husband. But she is too simple and guileless to know how to cut him short, or even how to conceal the superficial pleasure she gets from Vasenka's obvious admiration. Finally,

Levin makes the move. He leads Kitty out to the garden where they have a heated argument. Leaving her in tears, Levin seeks out his brother-in-law, Oblonsky. He is ashamed to tell him of his jealousy, but he feels he must. Oblonsky is shocked, not by the fact that Vasenka is infatuated with Kitty-something both he and Dolly had noticed-but the fact that Levin should be so jealous. He scolds him, "Most people would say Vasenka is behaving naturally... . A husband, who is a man of the world, should only be flattered by such behavior to a young and pretty wife."

Levin is not amused or persuaded. He goes to Veslovsky and tells him that he has ordered him a carriage. The young man is mystified, but watching Levin pick up a heavy stick, snap it in two and carefully catch one of the pieces as it falls, he recognizes that muscles speak more effectively than words. After receiving Oblonsky's apologies for Levin's actions, the young man departs.

Dolly carries out her intention to visit Anna. During the long drive over to the estate, Dolly has ample time to think about her problems. She recalls how she had been dismayed by a peasant woman who was relieved when God called home one of her many children. She asks herself whether she is any different. Her fifteen years of marriage have brought nothing but pregnancy, sickness, boredom, disfigurement, and finally, the death of her last born of croup. What was it all for? Her thoughts turn to Anna - Anna who had told her to stick to Stiva. In all honesty, Dolly admits she cannot reproach Anna for leaving Karenin. Anna did right; she is happy.

CHAPTERS 17 THROUGH 32

Before Dolly's carriage reaches the estate, it is joined on the road by four riders on horseback and two people in a new open carriage drawn by a magnificent black horse. Anna and Vasenka

Veslovsky are the first two on horseback, followed by Vronsky and a jockey. In the carriage are the Princess Varvara, a poor aunt of Anna's who is always toadying to the rich, and Levin's landowner friend, Sviazhsky. Dolly is immediately struck by Anna's beauty-her black curls escaping from under a top hat and her slender waist in the black riding habit. She is even more impressed by the easy grace with which Anna dismounts unaided and runs over to her. Dolly is huddled in the corner of Levin's old vehicle with its ill-matched horses.

Anna climbs in with her. Dolly feels that the happiness her trip is bringing Anna makes it worthwhile. She is glad to hear Anna say that she is contented, in spite of her position. Vronsky, she declares, has turned into a first rate landlord, reckoning every penny in his management. This becomes evident to Dolly when she sees the improvements he has made on his property. The guest room was furnished with more luxury than Dolly had ever known. She was ashamed to have the maid unpack her one, best dress. This sumptuousness is even carried to the nursery where Dolly requests Anna to take her. The little Ani, having her dinner in a tiny little armchair, is flanked by go-carts from England, a walking machine (she is just beginning to crawl), swings, and novel kinds of baths. In attendance are a Russian nursemaid, a wet nurse, and an English head nurse. It saddens Dolly when she begins to realize that Anna's visits to the child are not too frequent.

Although Dolly tells herself she approves of the step Anna has taken, she thinks that Vronsky's pride rests on nothing but his wealth. However, as he takes the trouble to show off his home and the hospital he has built, Dolly begins to recognize how hard he works at his projects. He is so eager for her to admire his efforts that she begins to see how Anna can be in love with him. Leading her apart from the others, Vronsky obviously wants to ingratiate himself with Dolly. When he explains how grateful he is that she, alone of Anna's friends and relatives, has come for a visit, Dolly suddenly becomes aware that he is counting on her for something. Her impression is confirmed when he tries to persuade her to influence Anna to write to Karenin for a divorce. After all, it was Dolly's Stiva who had practically arranged this before. In telling Dolly that he knows he is to blame for all Anna's suffering, he also makes it clear how important the divorce is to him. "My daughter is by law not my daughter, but Karenin's.... Someday we may have a son. He would not be heir to my name.... I have found occupation and am proud of what I am doing.... I want to know what I am doing will not die with me."

At the end of this impassioned plea, Dolly consents to talk to Anna. A sumptuous dinner intervenes. Watching Anna gaily enjoying what is put before her, Dolly understands that the planning of the household is as much Vronsky's job as the management of the estate. Anna is hostess only in the guidance of the conversation. She performs this duty naturally, and with her usual tact. Speaking lightly, Anna creates an atmosphere of impersonality at the dinner. Dolly dislikes such formality.

Dolly is in bed when Anna comes for the talk they both have wanted, but have been delaying subconsciously. Minutes pass before Dolly gets around to saying, "I think you ought to get married." Anna, interpreting the remark to mean that her "irregular position" is causing difficulties for the rest of the family, is offended. Dolly, ignoring Anna's sullenness, explains that she is pleading for Ani, for Vronsky, and his children. At the mention of children, Anna looks away, closes her eyes and says that she does not wish to have any more children. Dolly is shocked, but she remembers the thoughts she allowed herself in the carriage that same morning. How different is Anna's reasoning! Dolly realizes that Anna wants to keep her figure and to be healthy, for one purpose only-to hold Vronsky. She is afraid that he will leave her.

Nevertheless, Dolly persists in advising Anna to take steps so that she can marry him. Anna admits that when she contemplates writing to Karenin, she nearly goes mad and has to take morphine to get sleep. She is no longer sure that Karenin will still give her a divorce, now that he is under the influence of Countess Ivanovna. If he did, he would keep Seriozha; of this Anna is now sure. The confession that she needs Seriozha as much as she needs Vronsky brings her to tears.

Autumn finds Anna and Vronsky alone in the country without visitors. Still no steps have been taken toward a divorce, Anna spends much of her time reading subjects she knows are of interest to her lover. Vronsky would be content if he did not have to expect a scene every time he has to absent himself for business, local sessions, or the races. In October, the elections in Kashin province are scheduled. (This province includes the estates of Vronsky, Oblonsky, and Levin.) Vronsky, bracing himself for a rebuke, informs Anna of his intention to go. Instead of the usual argument followed by a reconciliation, merely silence and coldness ensue. This worries Vronsky when he leaves.

In contrast to Vronsky's desire for a change is Levin's reluctance to go to Kashin, even though he has trusteeship business there. Kitty urges him to participate. When Koznyshev adds his insistence, Levin agrees. After six days, while the sessions are going on, his attempts to do business grind to a halt. He enjoys talking to the older noblemen who feel they must keep on running their estates, even at a loss, because they have a duty to the property of their ancestors. Politics is beyond Levin's comprehension. He is aware that there are two parties, an old one and a new one. At the balloting, Levin could not really get the point, because many old men belonged to the new party and many young men to the old. When Koznyshev pulls him out of the little restaurant where he has gone to escape the confusion, he puts his ball in the wrong side of the ballot box.

Vronsky, on the other hand, enjoys the session. He finds the political fights exciting. He takes up his duties with enthusiasm. His influence, favored by the fact that the governor is a former schoolmate, assures his success. Regardless of the fact that the sessions have been extended, he takes time to give a victory dinner for his favorite candidate. Just as his guests are rising from the table, he receives a telegram from Anna. She says that she is frantic, that Ani is sick, that she expected him two days before, and that she has thought of coming herself to find out what he is doing. Vronsky is dumbfounded by the contradiction between the child's illness and her idea of leaving her to come to him. Much as he is reluctant to forego the election festivities, innocent as they are, he takes the first train home.

During his absence, Anna tried to fill her days with various activities, but at night she tormented herself with the idea that Vronsky's love was beginning to cool. Since marriage would be the one way to hold him, she tried to bring herself to the point of writing to Karenin for a divorce. Because she didn't do this, she was sleepless and turned to morphine. She is ashamed because of the telegram and dreads how Vronsky will greet her. On his arrival Vronsky is glad that the baby is well again, whereas Anna is almost sorry the recovery has been so speedy. He asks, "Anna, why are you so irritable? Don't you know I can't live without you?"

"If so," says Anna, "it must mean that you are sick of this life… . Yes, you will come home for a day, and then go off again the way men always do… . If you go to Moscow, I shall come too. I shall not stay here alone. Either we must separate or else live together all the time." Vronsky explains that this has always been his desire.

Soon after this, Anna writes to her husband about the divorce. Expecting an answer everyday, they go to Moscow, not to a hotel where they have separate apartments, but to housekeeping as a married couple.

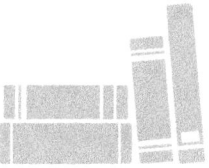

ANNA KARENINA

TEXTUAL ANALYSIS

PART SEVEN

CHAPTERS 1 THROUGH 16

At the insistence of the Princess Shcherbatsky, the Levins take a house in Miscow so that Kitty will have more than a country midwife to help when the baby comes. Because their calculations are wrong, they are still waiting after two months. Levin, besides being irked by inactivity, is also upset by their additional expenses in Miscow. For the first time, Levin has no money in the bank and is forced to sell his wheat at a low price. To pass the time, Levin does a little work on his book and discusses it with various intellectuals. No one seems able to talk about agriculture except in terms of capital, wages, and rent; the importance of the Russian peasant is completely forgotten. Nevertheless, Levin enjoys the talk and makes many new friends. Kitty, recognizing her husband's restlessness, urges him to get out as much as possible. Fortunately, he enjoys music and going to concerts.

More enjoyable is the club. Levin had long since given up his own membership, but is appreciative when his father-in-law puts his name down. It is pleasant to know that the hall porter and many of the members still know who he is. On one occasion he is hailed to a table by Turovtsin, who had livened up the dinner on the night he wrote chalk letters to Kitty. Later, Vronsky and Oblonsky join them. They enjoy talking ribald stories over several rounds of champagne. Levin, who had been abrupt with Vronsky during the election at Kashin, congratulates him on the first prize one of his horses won that day. Levin is pleased to discover how congenial Vronsky is. Before long they seem to have much in common, in particular their cattle. When Oblonsky gathers that any previous animosity between the two men has disappeared, he suggests that Vronsky take Levin to see Anna. Vronsky is delighted at the proposal, even though he feels that he must stay to watch over Yashin, his former roommate who is gambling too much. Levin hesitates for a moment, but his giddy condition eventually leads him to agree.

In the carriage on the way to Anna's Levin begins to wonder "What will Kitty say?" He is only half-listening to Oblonsky, who is explaining that Anna's divorce has been dragging on for months, and that there are difficulties about the son. He is not truly aware of where he is until he finds himself on the staircase of Anna's house, facing the portrait that Mihailov had painted. The lovely woman "with the black curling hair, bare shoulders and arms and a dreamy smile on her soft, downy lips," fascinates him.

"I am delighted," says Anna. In reality, thinks Levin, she is less dazzling than the portrait. But he is at once aware of something fresh and seductive in the living woman that the portrait did not capture. Speaking easily and without haste, she makes him feel comfortable. Soon they are talking about an exhibit that both had recently visited. When their talk turns to literature, Zola and Daudet hold their attention. She explains that books are one of the ways she keeps occupied. Before he leaves, Levin notices that a certain rigidity comes over Anna's face when she talks about herself. Though he thinks she is still beautiful, he feels sorry for her.

Self-pity prompts Anna to scold Vronsky when he returns. Pacing the room after Levin leaves, she quickly forgets him, even though she knows she has succeeded in arousing him. She has done it to amuse herself, to pass the time, like taking morphine. She wipes her tears away and is trying to look calm when Vronsky enters. Another one of their scenes ensues. She scolds; he pleads guilty. He surrenders, and when forgiven, immediately forgets his surrender. Anna is frightened by the discord that seems to be growing side by side with their love. Kitty is not pleased with the way Levin spent his evening, but she knows full well that it was unusual, so she forgives him. She even lets him sleep two hours after her labor begins. It is seven in the morning when she wakes him.

The day Levin's child is born is a day without time for him. He, the unbeliever, has a prayer on his lips from morning to night. It is more than twelve hours later when the nurse holds up his son and congratulates him on the "beautiful baby," who does not strike him as being at all beautiful.

CHAPTERS 17 THROUGH 31

When Oblonsky's affairs are in a bad way, he seeks an additional job that will pay well. His chance at the job rests in the hands of influential friends in St. Petersburg; among them are Karenin and the Countess Ivanovna. Oblonsky goes to Karenin to sponsor his cause and is coldly received. Karenin seems to enjoy being in a position to turn him down. Oblonsky, summoning all his courage and making the best of his charm, tries to ignore Karenin's effrontery and then makes a plea for Anna's divorce. Karenin shouts that he has no interest in Anna and that the divorce is a dead matter, because Anna wants to take his son away from him. When reminded that he had once generously agreed to divorce, Karenin says he had no right to make such a promise. Now that he has become a man of God, he cannot go against the teaching of the church. When Oblonsky begs him to exercise the Christian spirit of forgiveness, Karenin is forced to reflect, and promises an answer the next day.

Thinking to enhance his cause, Oblonsky proceeds that same day to the Countess Lydia Ivanovna. When he is announced, he is ushered into a drawing-room where she is seated at a small table talking to Karenin. After greeting Oblonsky, she introduces a short, thin-bodied man who comes out from a dark corner. It is Monsieur Landau. Oblonsky had heard of the Frenchman because he had been adopted by the Countess Bezzubov, who had met him in Paris. The story is that one day Landau, a simple shop assistant, had fallen asleep in a doctor's office. In his sleep he had given advice to other patients. All were cured. Then he cured the Countess, who brought him to Russia. Knowing this story, Oblonsky is curious, but after a few minutes of watching the Princess Ivanovna fawn over this oddity, he begins to fidget. He realizes that the timing of his call is wrong. It would be a mistake to make any pleas for himself or for Anna. However, the Countess brings the conversation around to Anna's problems. She tells him what a wonderful change has come over Karenin, now that he understands the Sacred Truth. The implication is that Karenin is now so sinless that he can be happy that God has removed Anna from his life. She then begins to read from a book in English called *Safe and Happy or Under the Wing*.

Monsieur Landau is asleep, pretending to be, or is in a trance. Oblonsky feels he must leave as quickly as possible. He does so, almost rudely. When, the next morning, he receives Karenin's flat refusal to divorce Anna, he knows the decision was based on one of the Frenchman's "messages."

Later in the spring, when Moscow is becoming hot and dusty, Anna and Vronsky are still in their furnished house. They have waited for six months for the divorce. Both are miserable. Both would prefer being in the country. Anna is alone very often. She imagines that Vronsky is unfaithful. She finds herself jealous of the young Princess Sorokin, because Vronsky remarked that his mother once wanted him to marry her. Even though she knows in her heart that Vronsky has no interest in this girl or any woman other than herself, she is quarrelsome. There are a series of quarrels that try Vronsky's patience. "It has its limits," he tells her. She imagines their affair is over and decides she must kill herself.

Back in her own room, she wonders if this is the final quarrel or whether another reconciliation is possible. She begins to imagine all the different feelings he will have after she is dead. The sound of approaching footsteps arouses her. Pretending not to hear him, she lets Vronsky come close to her. There is a look of tenderness in his eyes. Instantly her despairing jealousy is changed to loving passion. She throws her arms around him and covers his head, his neck and hands with kisses.

They agree to return to the country. At first she wants to go at once, but he has promised to see his mother, who is a short distance from town. The mention of his mother puts Anna in a bad mood again. She is still jealous of the girl his mother called to his attention. When he explains that he needs to see his mother about their property, to sign some papers and transfer some money, he tries to make other arrangements. She is left alone again all day. Before going to bed, she tells the maid to tell him that she has a headache and that he should not come to her room when he comes in. The maid carries out her instructions, and so does Vronsky. In the meantime, Anna has said to herself, "If he comes in spite of the maid's message, it means he loves me still. If he doesn't, it means that all is over, and then I shall know what to do.... ." After she hears him come in, she pours her usual dose of opium and thinks that she has only to swallow the whole bottleful to die. Horror falls upon her. To escape her panic, she hurries down to his room. He is sound asleep. At the sight of him, she cannot restrain her tears. She loves him, but she is afraid that if she wakes him, he will look at her coldly with self-righteousness while she explains. Without waking him, she slips back to her room.

The next morning when she hears a carriage stop, Anna runs to the window where she sees a young girl giving instructions to a footman. She hears Vronsky run down the steps. Hatless, he goes up to the carriage, talks to the girl and smiles. She hands him a packet and the carriage drives off. Anna is in a jealous rage again. She scarcely listens when he says that the Princess Sorokin and her daughter had merely come to deliver the money and documents from his mother. He is exasperated. He decides that all he can do is to take no notice. Accordingly, he prepares to go out. He has to see his mother in any case; he needs a power-of-attorney. Vronsky has scarcely left when Anna asks the servant where he has gone. When she learns that he is at the stables, she writes a note which is to be sent after him. "It's all my fault. Come back home. We must talk things over. For God's sake come. I'm frightened."

The note does not reach Vronsky. The servant tells her that he could not catch up with him. He has gone to the station.

Believing that he has gone to his mother's, she sends the man there with a second note. This she follows with a telegram. "I absolutely must talk to you. Come at once."

While waiting, she does not know what to do with herself. Afraid to be alone, she decides to visit Dolly. There she finds Kitty, who has been very sick since the birth of her baby. At first Dolly receives Anna alone. When Anna deliberately asks her whether Kitty is avoiding her, Dolly is shocked. Kitty, who has been nursing the baby, soon joins them. She is kind to Anna, who is embarrassed and does not stay long. "She's just the same, and as attractive as ever," Kitty says to Dolly, after Anna has gone. "How beautiful she is! But there is something pitiful about her, terribly pitiful!"

"Yes, there's something peculiar about her today," agrees Dolly. "When I was seeing her out, I fancied she was almost crying."

Still having received no answers several hours later, Anna is more distraught. She decides to go to the railway station. If she can't find him there, she will go to the house herself. She looks up the timetable, orders the carriage, packs a small traveling case and sets out. There is a large jostling crowd in the noisy station. She forgets for a moment where she is. Her coachman buys her ticket and settles her in a compartment. There are other occupants. After the train pulls out, she imagines they are making remarks for her benefit. One lady says, obviously pleased with her French, "Reason has been given to man to enable him to escape from his troubles." The remark fits Anna's reflections.

At her station, Anna gets off and, in the grimy crowd of ugly people, has difficulty recollecting why she has come. By accident, she learns that a coachman has come to meet the

Princess Sorokin and her daughter. As she is talking, Vronsky's coachman, rosy-faced and pleased with himself, hands her a note. She tears open the message, "Very sorry your note did not reach me. I shall be back at ten."

Very quietly, she dismisses the coachman and starts to walk along the platform past the station buildings. "No I won't let you torture me." In a flash she remembers the man who had been run down by the train the first day she met Vronsky. She knows what to do. A sensation similar to the feeling she always has when bathing, before she takes the first plunge, seizes her. She crosses herself. At exactly the moment when the space between the wheels draws level with her, she throws aside her bag, drops her head between her shoulders, and sinks to her knees. At the same instant, she is horror-struck at what she is doing. "Where am I? What am I doing? Why?" She tries to get up, to throw herself back; but something huge and relentless strikes her. Drags her down. "God forgive me everything."

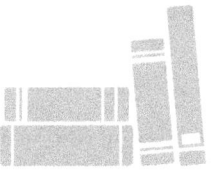

ANNA KARENINA

TEXTUAL ANALYSIS

PART EIGHT

Some two months after Anna's death, Vronsky recovers sufficiently to go back into the army. He is not returning however, to the dashing life of horse-racing, gambling and high society that he had known as a rich and titled officer. He is going into action. Although officially the imperial government has not recognized the war between the Serbians and the Turks, sympathy for the Serbs is mounting. Many prominent Russians are making subscriptions to help finance the Serbian effort. The press, controlled by the intellectuals, continues the appeal for volunteers. Not only does Vronsky join up, but he is taking along a whole squadron at his own expense.

At the railroad station bands are playing. Songs are echoing from one corner to another. Girls are throwing bouquets to their sweethearts. Society ladies are soliciting donations. The Princess Myagky is sending a thousand rifles and twelve nurses. Oblonsky is there in high spirits; he cannot resist putting a five-ruble note into the collection box of one of the young ladies.

He seems to have entirely forgotten how he sobbed over his sister's coffin. Many of his friends are milling about. He bumps into Koznyshev and his argumentative companion Katavasov. Koznyshev is traveling part way on the troop train. It is time for his summer visit with Levin. When Oblonsky hears this, he tells Koznyshev to tell Dolly, who is staying with Kitty and Levin, that everything is all right. By this he means he got the job with the high salary. As the bell rings, Oblonsky escapes into the crowd moving to the door.

"There he is!" Vronsky, in a long coat and black broad-brimmed hat, is walking in with his mother on his arm. He looks straight ahead with a frown on his face. He has aged. Going up to the train, he lets his mother step in before him, and vanishes into the compartment. On the platform "God Save the Tsar" is struck up.

Koznyshev's restlessness and intellectual curiosity propel him, to take a walk through the train. The volunteers, he learns, are not a heroic group of young men cheerfully doing their duty. They are a rowdy lot, drunk or already sleeping off their stupor. From a few fragmentary conversations, they appear to be largely society's misfits and failures, runaways from home, women, debts, or disgrace of some sort. At one of the train stops, Koznyshev, glad for a breath of air, sees the old Countess Vronsky who is traveling part way just in order to be a while longer with her son. She urges him to talk to the solitary figure walking up and down "like a caged animal, turning sharply every twenty paces." Vronsky cannot help recalling the last time he was called to a railway platform. He sees the lovely face, the black curls around the temples, the red half-open lips, the dreadful expression reminding him of their last quarrel. His mental anguish is interrupted by the awareness of acute physical pain. He has an excruciating toothache.

Koznyshev again arrives at the estate at its busiest season. Levin, as much as he looks forward to his brother's visits, begrudges the time spent on intellectual discussions and seemingly endless arguments, which he usually loses. Levin has been indulging in too many arguments with himself. He still adores Kitty, but she is very much occupied with the new baby and his demands. In addition, her sister and her sister's children have multiplied the household problems. Her activity brings her happiness and peace. Levin, though happy, is not at peace with himself.

He is often discouraged by his failures to help the lot of his peasants and by his financial losses on the estate; he finds himself asking more and more, "What is life all about?" He alternates between driving himself physically and battling with extensive philosophical reading. The unbeliever, who prayed so ardently during Kitty's confinement, has returned to unbelief. The little baby is but one more member of a bustling household. Kitty's efficient, thoughtful attentions to everyone remind him of her competent handling of his brother's last illness. Nikolai's death remains very real to him. Death is a fact of life he finds difficult to comprehend. Must he really die? He actually hides a rope for fear of the temptation to use it.

Levin has scarcely greeted Koznyshev and Katavasov on their arrival, when he notices that Kitty is not about. When he learns from Dolly that she has taken Mitya (the baby) to a nearby wood because it was too hot indoors, Levin is annoyed. He has often advised Kitty that he believed the woods dangerous. Soon after, a cloud turns black. A wind springs up. When it becomes as dark as during an eclipse, a down-pour seems imminent. Snatching up some rugs, Levin rushes off to the woods. The wind keeps pushing him back. The lightning flashes and the thunder claps. In another flash he sees a big oak crash down.

"Oh my God, my God! If only it's not on them." Pushing himself forward, slashing through the wet, he suddenly realizes he is praying. Is this senseless? Just the same he keeps on praying.

When he finds them alive, he thanks God. As he squeezes Kitty's hand, he knows that the meaning of life that he has been searching for has been staring him in the face. The value of living, of staying alive, is so simple to understand. It is clear that he has been thinking badly but living right.

They return to the house. The new feeling of peace and happiness that is engulfing Levin is soon broken by Kitty's preoccupation with the trivial details of housekeeping. Levin gradually apprehends, to his disappointment, how little the new feeling has changed him. Life still has its momentum. He will go on fighting for the estate, getting angry at the laborers, go on reading and arguing, continue to express himself badly, keep on blaming his wife for small things, go on not understanding why he prays, but praying anyway. But, he knows that from now on his life will not be as meaningless as it was before. He is aware of the power of living right, of the power of goodness. Levin sees what Anna had ignored: one must live for others and for God, not for oneself-real love is self-sacrifice, not self-assertion for one's own gain.

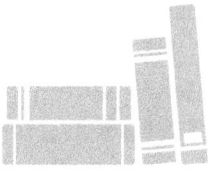

ANNA KARENINA

CHARACTER ANALYSES

It has been said that there are no minor characters in *Anna Karenina*. Many people enter into the story and Tolstoy, like Adam, gave them all-at least most-names. Each comes to life as a result of some tell-tale characteristic that distinguishes him from the class of people who mingle in the streets of St. Petersburg or travel over the countryside. The paths of some cross those of others. It is out of these confluxes that Tolstoy has woven his story. There are six people whose journeys cross and recross so many times, whose relationships are so much more complicated, and more tragic, that they can be singled out as the major actors in this drama.

These six are:

1. Oblonsky
2. Levin
3. Kitty
4. Vronsky
5. Anna
6. Dolly

Two points should be noticed about this list: first is the sequence of the numbers assigned to the characters, and second is the fact that Karenin fails to appear on the list.

Number one and number six, Oblonsky and his wife Dolly, enclose the others. In a sense they represent the social setting. They are the grownup children of upper-class nineteenth century Russia that Count Tolstoy was born into and is describing-if not admiring. Number one and number two are both men, and at the other end of the list, number five and six are both women. Levin, Oblonsky's friend, has little good to say about him; he finds his way of life repulsive, with its sensuousness, its compromises and its acceptances. Dolly, number six, though forgiving her husband's behavior, cannot condone Anna's way of life - the way that brazenly ignores society's codes. On the list, Anna is on one side of Vronsky and Kitty is on the other. Kitty is the pretty girl, the wife and mother who is so engrossed by what is close and dear to her that society swims past her, including Vronsky. Vronsky, himself, represents high society; he is a member of the Russian nobility. He is the incarnation of its manners and its codes; as such, he foreshadows its doom, a doom prophesied by Tolstoy and witnessed in our time.

OBLONSKY

Prince Oblonsky is Stiva to his family and his many friends, all of whom love him, or at least he thinks they do. He certainly is likable; his good spirits are infectious. He knows the waiters and the hatcheck girls of all the smart places of St. Petersburg and Moscow. He knows how to entertain without giving the impression that extravagances must be paid for. A charmer, he can nearly always wheedle a little extra credit. Because he is friendly, he is a success at his job at the law courts that a relative-in the last instance, Karenin-was influential enough to procure for him. He is at home at the club, drinking and telling stories. A lover of sports, he follows the races, hunts, and is an exceptional shot. Besides taking pleasure in the theatre, actresses and ballerinas, he can appreciate folk music and peasant girls. In the case of the latter, he considers that adventures into infidelity are manly. Moreover, he can still love his wife and family. The nuisance of money is the sad part of his life. Money is his tragedy; at the close of the novel he stoops for money by taking a job outside of his class-a class whose members are supposed to live chiefly from their estates. He is forced, because of his debts, to swallow his pride and seek the support of those beneath him. Nonetheless, he is to be admired because he can, and does, sell himself into the post. He is at the last seen at the railway station, among friends, distributing largess, humming with the bands, cheering the soldiers, smoothing his whiskers, forgetful of his problems. "With all his faults, one must do him justice," the princess remarked to Koznyshev as soon as Oblonsky had left them. "He has the true Russian, Slav nature!"

LEVIN

The other half of the true Russian is Tolstoy's autobiographical character, Levin. Many of the events that happen to Levin in *Anna Karenina* happened to the author also. The scene where the shy Levin cannot bring himself to speak to Kitty, but writes down the first letters of the words he cannot articulate, is a reproduction of Tolstoy's proposal to his wife. And Levin, like Tolstoy, was a wealthy young count who had not lived a chaste and innocent life, and felt he must give his diary to his sweetheart. The difference between Oblonsky and Levin is clearly marked by the fact that Oblonsky enjoys his sensuality and Levin regrets his. Levin is much too sensitive to ignore the "other partner."

His humanity is more extensive; he feels he must help the other fellow. How to do this? Here reason takes over. He must think, plan, study, and learn, in order to understand. In his effort to comprehend the meaning of life, he exerts all his mental powers. As a result, his heart and his head are often in conflict. His heart says, "Give all that you don't need to the peasant." His mind has to admit that the peasant is so set in his ways that he distrusts the giver and will destroy his gift. His heart says, "I need help, and may God give it to me." His minds asks what proof there is of God's existence.

Of one thing he is certain; he is in love with Kitty. He recognizes his love as a force greater than himself. His emotional commitment is so complete that he is excessively jealous. This jealousy becomes a tragic flaw. At one point it makes a comic of him, when he rudely sends Vasenka away. The young lad could not help being innocently aroused by Kitty's beauty, young motherhood, and unconscious acknowledgment of his attentions. Kitty is annoyed by her husband's display of jealousy, but loves him the more for it. It is Kitty's love, more than books, religion, sport or work, that saves Levin's sanity. He learns his lesson through her; love makes the physical aspects of life lose their grossness. Because of love, life can sometimes be beautiful, and the certainty of death can be endured.

KITTY

If Levin is Tolstoy, one speculates on similarities between Kitty and Tolstoy's wife. The fictional character and the real woman were both a great deal younger than their husbands. Both had older sisters who were often on hand with their children. Both were practical and knew how to manage a complicated household. Both had tempers, not hesitating to scold their husbands. Both were soon pregnant after marriage. Here the comparison ends, because at the end of *Anna Karenina*, Kitty and Levin are still a young couple with one child. However, it is well within the reach of imagination to picture Kitty as the older Countess Tolstoy, who later became the mother of many children and the watchdog of money, as her husband became more and more improvident and religious.

VRONSKY

The reader meets Vronsky before Vronsky meets Anna. It is important that Vronsky be seen as a dashing young officer, as an aristocrat, almost classified with the other popinjays whom Kitty's father says St. Petersburg turns out by the dozen. By the dozen, yes, but Vronsky's frosting is a little thicker; he is richer; more gallant, more sure of himself, more reckless, more proud, and more highly bred. Undoubtedly his affair with Anna changes him. Tolstoy's characters do not "develop"; their changes are on the surface. A man's basic character is formed early. Though the momentum of life acts upon Vronsky and he reacts, the degree of the reaction is almost predictable. What people do to him and what he does to people are but outgrowths of his basic essence.

The six **episodes** at railway stations are the most revealing. In the first, he goes as a dutiful son to meet his wealthy mother who is traveling with her major-domo, her maid and her lapdog. More interesting than his mother is the beautiful young woman who shared her compartment, Madame Karenina. Vronsky does not consider for a moment that she is a married woman or that he knows her husband, high government official. He is not really listening to his mother when she comments that she and Anna have spent the journey in talking about their sons. Rather he sees her only as a woman and makes her realize this. He immediately tries to capture her affection by being overly generous and dramatic when the trainman is killed. The next time he sees her at a railway station is when she has run away from him. She does not trust herself to see more of him in Moscow. She is on her way back to her husband in St. Petersburg. When she gets off at an in-between stop, she is surprised by him. She had no idea he was on the same train. He declares his love and commits himself entirely to her: The reader knows that this young man, because he is an aristocrat who lives by the rigid codes of the aristocracy, will never go back on his promises to her. This frightens her. The next morning at the St. Petersburg terminal she is met by Karenin, who is unable to dismiss the young man. When she sees the two men together, both named Alexei, Anna knows her life is consigned to Vronsky.

On the day of Anna's suicide, Vronsky was once more attending to his mother's business. He had money matters to handle for her. According to his code, he treated his mother in ways he did not believe interfered with his treatment of Anna. Although he was influenced by his mother, who felt that Anna was ruining his life, he never went back on his promises to Anna. From the beginning of their affair he was willing to let Karenin point a loaded pistol at him while he shot into the air. In fact, he despised Karenin for his cowardice. For Anna's sake, he lived openly with her, but he knew that society would crush her. He knew his world better than she. He recognized that her wishful thinking was dishonest, but he was committed to her. There was no going back. Accordingly he always gave in. In spirit, however, if not indeed, he was dishonest. In his innermost depths he knew he was not entirely committed; he felt he must keep some independence. He must have some life apart from her-estate management, politics, sport, horses, training and exercise. In believing that he still had a right to these, he deceived himself and thereby made Anna a lonely woman - the woman for whom, he told himself, he had given up all. And so, when he was called to the railway station to identify her body, he thought he had lost everything. Nevertheless, his story does not end here. In Part Eight Tolstoy provided an epilogue. One sees Vronsky again at the Railway station. Within two months, he has signed up with many other misfits to fight in the Serbian war.

He tells Koznyshev that he does not care whether or not he loses his life on the battlefield. But does he believe in his own death? Does this young man, whose life is still making headlines, realize that he is still playing a role? Is he behaving according to his code? Tolstoy does not tell us directly, but by pointing out that Vronsky has a toothache, the author diminishes some of the value and force of the aristocratic code. Tolstoy is predicting the downfall of the Russian aristocracy.

ANNA

Anna is the victim of the society Vronsky represents - the society her brother Stiva compromises with and thereby betrays, the society Kitty avoids and Levin transcends. Anna, an orphan, was raised under the guardianship of an autocratic and domineering aunt. The aunt wanted a brilliant match for her young niece, and was able to maneuver Karenin into marriage. Anna tried to be a dutiful wife. Of course, her beauty guaranteed her acceptance in social circles helpful to Karenin. Her initial fascination with this sort of life soon turned to boredom, when she became familiar with its intrigues. Meanwhile she had a son. She showered all the affection on this boy which her husband had been unable to tap. Seriozha, in his turn, worshipped her to the exclusion of his busy father.

When she goes to Moscow in an attempt to patch up her brother's troubles with Dolly, she leaves her son for the first time. Although she has long been free of her husband spiritually, she is now free from her son's presence physically. She sees in Vronsky a promise of something she is momentarily free to accept. Since she is away from home, a flirtation appears harmless enough. At first she does not comprehend that Vronsky is young, and also a sophisticated wealthy man of the world who is not to be teased. When she realizes that it is his very worldliness that attracts her, she is frightened. Later when she finds she loves Vronsky, she deceives herself into thinking that she can have both Vronsky and Karenin (by Karenin she subconsciously means his son). When she is aware of the great gulf between her husband and her son, she again deceives herself into thinking that Karenin will allow her to have both her lover and her son. After she gives birth to Vronsky's daughter, she further deceives herself by assuming that Karenin will forgive her. When Karenin goes back on his promise, she even assumes that society will repudiate him and forgive her.

All of these self-deceptions mean nothing so long as she has Vronsky, and she knows he loves her. He accordingly becomes the goal of her whole life; she lives every moment for him. She becomes jealous of his absences. She fails to understand his need to be away from her. She imagines he is deceiving her even as others-her husband, her relatives, her old friends-are deceiving her. When she can trust no one, she distrusts herself most. Eventually, she realizes that she has not been struggling against society, but against herself. For the first time she is honest with herself, but it is too late. A whole series of petty annoyances - an undelivered message, a stupid coach-man, a billboard sign, a nightmare, a chance recollection - combine to force her under the wheels of a train.

DOLLY

The last of the six is the most lovable. She is more honest with herself than any of the others. She knows her husband is deceiving her, but she also knows that she can do little about her problem because of financial difficulties and a concern for her children's future. Refusing to be victimized, as Anna was, she faces up to the situation. She decides to make the best of her troubles and live as she can. In public, therefore, she ignores what she knows in private. No one will ever know her suffering. This is her decision. In this sense, she is the true heroine of *Anna Karenina*.

KARENIN

Why was Karenin omitted from the list of the main characters? The answer rests in the fact that at both the beginning and end of the novel, Tolstoy considered him less than a man. At the opening he is an automaton. He has the soul, or what goes by that name, of a clerk. He is a member of Officialdom, a rustler of paper, a creator of problems whose solutions are designed to create more problems. He comes to life briefly, when his wife gives birth to another man's child. He honestly feels sorry for her. Pity would appear to be the one emotion that can stir him, but event his is short-lived. He is influenced again by officialdom and by pseudo-religion. He allows himself to be duped by a quack medium. It is a stroke of poetic justice that Karenin, a fakir among the living, is destroyed by another like himself.

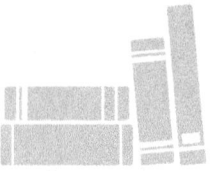

ANNA KARENINA

CRITICAL COMMENTARY

"I do not like *Anna Karenina*," wrote Tolstoy, "although there are in it some truly magnificent pages (the races, the harvest, the hunt). But all this is stale stuff, it reeks of Moscow, old maids, Slavicism, patricianism, and so forth."

The literary controversy that seems to survive from generation to generation and from one language to another is the question of the relative merit of *War and Peace* and *Anna Karenina*. On this subject it is perhaps worthwhile to quote the only contemporary Russian writer ever classed with Tolstoy-Dostoevsky. He wrote: "*Anna Karenina,* as an artistic product, is perfection…. Nothing in the literatures of Europe at the present time compares with it."

Marc Slonim, in *The **Epic** of Russian Literature*, shares this opinion:

In *Anna Karenina* the analysis of motivation and its moral impact are even more profound than in *War and Peace*. The construction of this psychological family novel is more harmonious than that of the historical **epic**, and this is particularly perceptible in the first part, where Tolstoy unfolds his plot by gradually shifting from secondary to more important incident, changing the whole scene, and planting at the very beginning all the concrete details that were to play a part in the **denouement** of the drama... . The writing of the novel coincided with the intensification of his (Tolstoy') inner conflicts, and therefore the identification of the story with the underlying moral idea is probably more thorough and obvious than in *War and Peace*: it gives to *Anna Karenina* a unity and a compactness that have made some critics proclaim it as Tolstoy's highest achievement. Although the plot again serves to show the flow of life, it is more of a story and so has more of a dramatic quality than the author's other works.

The Reader's Companion to World Literature comments: "The world of *Anna Karenina*, as Tolstoy creates it, is a slice of 19th-century Russia. Her tragedy is never quite raised from the limited social plane to a more symbolic or universal one. *War and Peace*, avowedly a historical novel, is still modern. *Anna Karenina*, at one time a 'modern' novel, has become historical."

REALISM IN ANNA KARENINA

Realism, as a recognizable literary creed, triumphed in the nineteenth century. It held that the purpose of art is to depict life with complete objectivity-to show things "as they really are." The realists avoided idealism and romantic treatment of subject matter. They often seemed to stress the commonplace (anti-heroic), the trivial, the sordid, or the brutal aspects as life as they saw it. Tolstoy is considered one of the greatest of the realistic novelists. He devoted himself to the milieu he knew best - the Russian nobility. A thorough realist, he included descriptions of himself and his life in *Anna Karenina*, sometimes not ever bothering to disguise them.

Commenting on the **realism** in Tolstoy's novels, Marc Slonim states:

He strictly observes the time element, the river-like quality of objective narrative; the even and majestic unrolling of his story which follows the natural sequence of events is completely contrary to the dramatic tenseness of Dostoevsky.... Particularly in *Anna Karenina* Tolstoy shows how everything fits into a large pattern, so that each of Anna's words and actions acquires significance and gains momentum as the novel progresses.... In Tolstoy the plot-as a combination of surprising incidents and accidents, as a complex entanglement of circumstances-hardly ever exists. For this anti-Romantic craftsman the processes of life, the progression of time, are in themselves sufficient vehicles for narration; a normal life-situation developing in a perfectly natural, almost banal, way offers him the pattern into which his **exposition** is woven.

Three of the best examples of realistic writing in *Anna Karenina* are the three passages which Tolstoy himself considered "magnificent" - the race, the harvest and the hunt. Most of the elements of the storyteller's genius are gathered together in the description of the events of the race. There are a series of minor conflicts that build up to Anna's declaration of war on her husband. Each step to the **climax** is structured and given unity through the artistic symbolism of the mare Frou-Frou. Tolstoy stretches the reader's patience with copious details - the racetrack crowd, Vronsky's visit to the stables, his visit to Anna in the garden, the four starts necessary to get the race underway, and the race itself. R. P. Blackmur, in *Eleven Essays in the European Nove*l, points out that Tolstoy foretells the entire outcome of the novel in the race scene: "What Vronsky wanted was Anna like the horse. But like the horse, Anna must be used in reckless pastime, or not at all. Take away the pastime and the recklessness becomes uncontrollable and all the beautiful anarchy in the animal-all the unknown order under orders known is lost. So, as with Anna, Vronsky failed to keep pace with Frou-Frou and broke her back."

G. P. Perris, in *Leo Tolstoy, the Grand Mujik: A Study in Personal Evolution*, calls the description of the harvest (Levin's day at the scythe with the laborers in Part III) "one of the crowning passages of modern literature." By means of cataloging the mundane details of mowing hay, Tolstoy is able to make of this commonplace day a spiritual experience for Levin.

Likewise, the hunt scene is outstanding because it is an amalgam of Tolstoy's art and his philosophy-his **realism** and his mysticism. He brings together three very different men-Vasenka, Oblonsky, and Levin - and teaches a valuable lesson in tolerance by exploring almost all of the human emotions The completeness of detail gives additional power to this realistic narrative passage.

CHARACTERIZATION

Tolstoy, like Shakespeare, is noted for the wide, almost limitless, range of his characterization. His psychological insight extended from landowners to peasants, from bureaucrats to mothers. Because of his devotion to both physical details and psychological motivation, the numerous characters in *Anna Karenina* are vitally alive, and highly individualized. Tolstoy's ability to penetrate the souls of women, particularly Anna's, has often been singled out for praise. He may have loved Anna,

Vronsky, and the other major figures in the novel, but devotion to psychological **realism** made him a relentless judge, who castigated weakness wherever he saw fit. The people in *Anna Karenina* are neither saints nor heroes; they are living human beings, often commonplace or confused, but very much alive.

TOLSTOY AS MORALIST

Though Tolstoy's devotion to **realism** leads one to expect him to attempt to be totally objective in *Anna Karenina*, he was not successful, particularly in the character of Levin. Anna contains no separate philosophical chapters (like those in War and Peace), but a very obtrusive moral philosophy is diffused throughout the story. It is generally puritan and can be felt as alien to the main groundwork of the novel. Anna suggests the moral and religious crisis that was influencing Tolstoy's own life at the time. His personal struggle colored his writings which barely disguised his polemical purpose. Like most Russian writers, he did not believe in art for art' sake; he longed to use literature to mold souls. Although his **didactic** extremism impairs the artistic merit of the novel at times, it would be unfair to label Tolstoy as a preacher. Primarily he was an artist, even though he lived to reject his own art in order to pursue the demands of moral asceticism.

"No novelist," wrote E. M. Forster in 1950 in *Aspects of the Novel*, "is as great as Tolstoy - that is to say has given so complete a picture of a man's life." In the same vein, George Steiner in *Tolstoy or Dostoevsky: An Essay in the Old Criticism* wrote: "the supreme poets of the world have been men impelled either to acquiescence or rebellion by the mystery of God, that there are magnitudes of interest and poetic force to which secular art cannot attain." Professor Steiner quotes D. H. Lawrence as saying, "One has to be so terribly religious, to be an artist."

If one agrees with this thesis, it is less difficult to understand Tolstoy's antipathy to Shakespeare and his affinity for Gandhi. Shakespeare, Tolstoy claimed, lacked a moral sense. Shakespeare suggests questions and answers to all of man's problems, and relations with other man, but avoids the fundamental question of man's destiny and his relationship with God. Unlike Shakespeare, Tolstoy had a desire, not to mirror the world but, to make the world better. To art he added a **didactic** ingredient. In later life he became a teacher with disciples, as Gandhi was. Because of his religious fervor, Tolstoy believed in the doctrine of non-resistance. To this movement, especially in one led by Gandhi in South Africa, Tolstoy gave generously, so generously that the farm Gandhi founded there in 1910 was called the "Tolstoy Farm." Characteristically this was a work farm. Tolstoy, the man and the artist, still believed in work-hard, physical labor, such as Levin's when "the sweat stood on his face and fell from his nose and all his back was wet."

ANNA KARENINA

ESSAY QUESTIONS AND ANSWERS

Question: Discuss the attendant moral issues raised by Anna's infidelity.

Answer: It has been said that Tolstoy did not want the reader to condemn Anna but to pity her. There was never a question of whether Anna was immoral - this was always the case in Tolstoy's mind. But he considered that ultimate judgment must rest with God, not with fallible men. This is the meaning of the epigraph to the novel, "Vengeance is mine; I will saith the Lord."

Tolstoy raised certain other moral questions too. The first is the subject of "arranged" marriages. Since Karenin had been chosen for Anna by a scheming relative, the moral blame for Anna's infidelity must be shared by others, including all upper class European society in the nineteenth century which encouraged the "marriage de convenance." There is a suggestion of this problem in the meditations of the old Princess Shcherbatsky, who had married off her two older daughters and was trying to arrange for Kitty. Had she been successful in pairing Kitty with Vronsky, would her act have been immoral? This is Tolstoy's question. He settles it by means of a masterly use of **irony**. Anna's immoral affair with Vronsky prevents an immorally-arranged marriage. True love, by its intervention, makes possible the moral love of Kitty and Levin.

A second question raised by Tolstoy is why society condemns Anna, while it allows Vronsky to go free. Tolstoy recognizes the "double standard" as a fact of life. To him the biological differences between male and female are inherent in this fact. It is, however, obvious that Tolstoy's sympathies are with Anna. Vronsky is a creation of his aristocratic class, and a rather weak one at that.

Another moral issue that becomes involved in Anna's infidelity concerns the church. Tolstoy's respect for the Russian state religion diminished increasingly during the time of his writing of *Anna Karenina*. This antipathy, which culminated later in his public excommunication, is obvious from the author's handling of Karenin, Anna's husband. As a member of the government, Karenin had to maintain his Christian orthodoxy. He initially ignores Anna's sin in order to prevent a scandal which would have embarrassed him as an official. Later, when her sin was no longer a secret, was he supposed, as a good Christian, to forgive, as Christ had forgiven? According to Tolstoy; the church said "no" to this. Karenin had no right to forgive, because he had no right to show approval of what the church disapproved.

Still another issue raised by Tolstoy concerned the rights of illegitimate children. Vronsky, as a count and a descendant of an old family wanted an heir. He would not give up Anna, even though any children he might have by her would be legally named Karenin. This problem raised still another, the complicated matter of Anna's decision not to have more children. In projecting this question, Tolstoy again shows the reader how far he was ahead of his time.

Question: Tolstoy is well known for certain "set pieces." By this expression is meant that action is staged in an elaborately theatrical way. Describe such a scene.

Answer: The wedding of Kitty and Levin is one of the most famous of such "set pieces." After a short description of the church with the crowds milling outside and the glitter of the candles within, the distinguished guests, the deacons, and the priests in purple vestments, Tolstoy describes the bride and bridegroom. What did the bride wear? Certainly everyone wants to know, but Tolstoy is too much an artist to supply the information as it might be found in the society columns of the Sunday Supplement. Instead Tolstoy describes the whole person. He walks around her. He views her with the eyes of several people. Somehow, by means of these piecemeal details, a full impression is achieved that is at once more personal and more lasting.

"Kitty, ready and waiting in her white dress, long veil, and wreath of orange blossom, stood in the drawing-room of the Shcherbatskys' house with her nuptial godmother and sister, Princess Lvov."

A whole chapter later the reader sees her as the bridegroom say her. "Everyone said she had lost her looks last few days, and on her wedding-day was nothing like so pretty as usual; but Levin did not find it so. He looked at her hair dressed high beneath the long weil and white flowers, at the high, stand-up, scalloped collar that in such a maidenly fashion had hid her long neck at the sides and just showed it a little in front, and at her strikingly slender waist, and it seemed to him she was more beautiful than ever - not because those flowers, the veil, or the gown from Paris added anything to her beauty, but because, in spite of the elaborate sumptuousness of her attire, the expression on her sweet face and lips was still that same look of hers of innocent truthfulness."

Two chapters later in the middle of the ceremony, we read: "'Put it right on!' was the advice heard from all sides when the priest brought forward the crowns and Shcherbatsky, his hand shaking in its three-button glove, held the crown high above Kitty's head."

At the end Levin did not know that the ceremony was over. "The priest came to his aid, saying softly, a smile on his kindly mouth, 'Kiss your wife, and you, kiss your husband,' and took the candles from their hands."

Question: Discuss the repetition of mannerisms to illuminate character.

Answer: "And, interlacing his fingers, palms downwards, he stretched them and the joints cracked... . This trick - the bad habit of clasping his hands and cracking his fingers-always soothed, and restored the mental balance so needful to him at this juncture."

Each time, and there are many, that Tolstoy had Karenin crack-his knuckles, the reader knows that Karenin is upset. This signal is minor in comparison to the reinforcement the reader gets of his understanding of Karenin. He is forced to ask himself, over and over again, what sort of man soothes and restores his equilibrium by such a gesture. How deeply was he "unsoothed" and "unbalanced?" It is unquestionable that Karenin loses statute every time he cracks his hands.

In the same sense, every time Anna squints as though she were trying to understand better, not what is merely in front of her but what is inside her, the reader loves her more. "Anna turned her eyes away from her friend's face and screwing them up (a new habit Dolly had not seen in her before) pondered... .

And Dolly saw that tears stood in her eyes. She pressed Anna's hand in silence."

Oblonsky has a trick of stroking his whiskers. The fact that they are beautifully curled gives him confidence. The reader learns that Oblonsky lives much on the surface. He is a hedonist. He runs away from life by stressing the superficial. Since life is tough, he keeps saying to himself, "gather ye rosebuds where ye may." The thickness of his mustache reinforces his belief that he is not too old for a rosebud.

Vasenka Veslovsky, the dashing young lad who does not seem to have a care in the world-who falls in love with Kitty and is thrown out because of it and who falls in love with Anna and is admired for it-has a habit of sitting down with one leg under him. This informal posture is characteristic of his entire nature, which is easy-going. Tolstoy's reiteration of this mannerism puts an indelible impression on the reader's visual memory.

Question: Describe an autobiographical **episode** other than Levin's proposal to Kitty.

Answer: Kitty's confinement, and the events of the day at the end of which she gives birth to her son, coincide with Tolstoy's personal experience.

"The princess, sitting at the other side of the table with the midwife and Oblonsky, called Levin to her and began talking about moving to Moscow for Kitty's confinement." In other words, the event was treated as a big family affair months in advance.

Some thirty chapters and several months later, Kitty "suffered, complained, triumphed, and rejoiced in her suffering, welcoming it. Something sublime was being accomplished in her soul, but what it was Levin could not understand. It was beyond his comprehension."

"'I have sent to Mama… . Kostya! … No, it's nothing. It's passed… . You go along now… . I am all right.' And to Levin's amazement, he saw her take up the knitting she had fetched in the night."

Almost immediately, Levin is jumping into a sledge and hurrying at daybreak for the doctor who is in no hurry whatsoever. "Won't you have a cup of coffee?" the doctor asked him. Levin "stared with eyes that asked if he was laughing at him. But the doctor had no idea of laughing at him."

"At five o'clock in the afternoon … Levin was asked to move a table and a couch. He did it with alacrity, imagining it was something for Kitty, and only later discovered that he had been preparing his own bed for the night … his heart was ready to burst with pity, and yet did not burst, and he prayed without pause to God. And everytime a scream from the bedroom aroused him … he would start up and run to justify himself, and remember on the way that he was not to blame and that he was only anxious to protect and help her. But when he looked at her, he saw once more that he could not help, and was filled with terror and repeated his prayer … the doctor put his head on one side, listened and smiled approvingly … a bold insistent, self assertive cry of the new human being… . It seemed to Levin too much, a superabundance, to which he was unable to get used for a long time."

Question: Why does Vronsky attempt suicide?

Answer: The deceived husband, Karenin, who had figured as a pitiful object, an incidental obstacle to Vronsky's happiness, had been changed by Anna, in the delirium of childbirth, to an elevated position. Instead of Karenin, Vronsky, the true father of the newborn, was abased. Abasement of any kind was a new sensation for this spoiled young aristocrat. His passion for Anna, which he thought had been on the point of cooling, was suddenly magnified. He felt he loved her more intensely than ever before. That his love was to be cut off forever was more than he could bear. The frustration drove the young man to insanity. He was exhausted and could not sleep. "What makes men," he asked, "lose their reason? What makes them shoot themselves?"

Even though his self-inflicted wound was a serious one, the point is that Vronsky survived. The madness of his attempt has a deliberate unreality. Levin's repeated battles with possible suicide are autobiographical as we know. They are part of the fabric of Tolstoy's own nature. The fact that Levin did not attempt what Vronsky accomplished effects the reader more powerfully.

Vronsky's "accident" also makes Anna's actual suicide more real and dramatic. Vronsky's attempt foreshadows the second event. Tolstoy clothes his description of it with a certain vagueness, although he makes sure the action is psychologically sound. Anna's self-destruction, on the other hand, based as it was on the actual suicide of one of Tolstoy's neighbors, leaves the reader with a psychological puzzlement. That Tolstoy purposely left the story unsettled in the finality of death is typical. He wants us to keep remembering Anna.

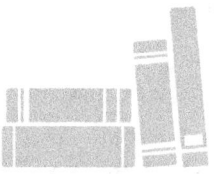

BIBLIOGRAPHY

Blackmur, R. P. *Eleven Essay in the European Novel*, New York, Harcourt, Brace & World, 1964.

Craufurd, Alexander H. *The Religion and Ethics of Tolstoy*, London, T. Fisher Unwin, 1912.

Davis, Helen E. *Tolstoy and Nietzsche*, New York, New Republic, Inc., 1929.

Garrod, H. W. *Tolstoy's Theory of Art*, Oxford, The Clarendon Press, 1935.

Hofmann, Modest and Andre Pierre. *By Deeds of Truth; The Life of Teo Tolstoy*, translated from the French by Ruth Whipple Fermaud, New York, The Orion Press, 1958.

Micek, Edward. *Tolstoy, The Artist and Humanist*, Austin, Texas, Czech Literary Society, 1961.

Noyes, George Rapall. *Tolstoy*, New York, Duffield & Company, 1918.

Perris, G. H. *Leo Tolstoy, The Grand Mujik: A Study in Personal Evolution*, Tendon, T. Fisher Unwin, 1898.

Phelps, William Tyon. *Essays on Russian Novelists*, New York, Macmillan, 1911.

Redpath, Theodore. *Tolstoy*, London, Bowes & Bowes, 1960.

Steiner, George. *Tolstoy or Dostoevsky*, New York, Alfred A. Knopf, 1959.

Tolstoy, Alexandra. *Tolstoy: A Life of My Father*, New York, Harper & Brothers, 1953.

Tolstoy, Leo. *Leo Tolstoy, His Life and Work: Autobiographical Material*, compiled by Paul Birukoff and revised by Teo Tolstoy, translated from the Russian, New York, Charles Scribner's Sons, 1906.

Tolstoy, Sergei. *Tolstoy Remembered, By His Son*, translated by Moura Budberg, London, Weidenfeld and Nicolson, 1962.

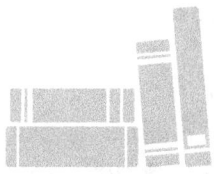

ANNOTATED BIBLIOGRAPHY

CHIEF WRITINGS OF TOLSTOY

Tolstoy wrote constantly and voluminously throughout his long life. The complete Soviet edition of his works, published from 1928-1959, runs to ninety volumes. Most of these are not available in English. Of those available the student should be aware of the following: *The Cossacks* (1863), *War and Peace* (1865-1869), especially in the translation by Louise and Aylmer Maude, available in a Simon and Shuster edition published in 1958, *Anna Karenina* (1875-1877), *A Confession* (1879), *The Death of Ivan Ilych* (1886), *The Kreutzer Sonata* (1889), *What is Art?* (1897), *The Resurrection* (1899), *Hadji Murad* (1896-1904).

CRITICISM

All told there is not a vast amount of criticism of Tolstoy in English. The student will find the following helpful: Matthew Arnold, "Count Leo Tolstoy," *Essays in Criticism, Second Series* (1888); Isaiah Berlin, *The Hedgehog and the Fox* (1953); Janks Lavin, *Tolstoy: An Approach* (1944); Thomas Mann, "Goethe and Tolstoy," *Essays of Three Decades* (1944); Philip Rahv, "Tolstoy:

The Green Twig and Black Trunk," *Images and Ideas*, (1949); George Steiner, *Tolstoy or Dostoevsky* (1959); Stefan Zweig, *Adepts in Self Portraiture: Casanova, Stendhal, Tolstoy* (1952). R. F. Christian's *Tolstoy's "War and Peace": A Study* (1962) is the best available study of the novel's sources, its conception and development, its publication history, and its narrative and character techniques.

BIOGRAPHY

Leo Tolstoy by Ernest J. Simmons (1949) is considered to be the best and fullest biography of the author. In addition to Simmons' work on Tolstoy's life, the student will find these from one point of view or another: P. I. Birgukov, *The Life of Tolstoy* (1911); Derrick Leon, *Tolstoy: His Life and Work* (1944); Alymer Maude, *The Life of Tolstoy*, 2 vols. (1908–1810); Alexandra Tolstoy, *Tolstoy: A Life of My Father* (1953).

www.ingramcontent.com/pod-product-compliance
Lightning Source LLC
LaVergne TN
LVHW011721060526
838200LV00051B/2989